New Dawn Within

To loving and living your best life

By Divneet Kaur

◆ FriesenPress

Suite 300 - 990 Fort St
Victoria, BC, V8V 3K2
Canada

www.friesenpress.com

Copyright © 2021 by Divneet Kaur
First Edition — 2021

ISBN
978-1-03-910631-4 (Hardcover)
978-1-03-910630-7 (Paperback)
978-1-03-910632-1 (eBook)

1. SELF-HELP, PERSONAL GROWTH

Distributed to the trade by The Ingram Book Company

Table of Contents

This book is dedicated to the three most important people in my life: my mother, who taught me to be self-reliant; my father, who taught me to be practical; and my husband, who taught me to love.

Introduction

Not to sound like an online dating profile, but I am a twenty-nine-year-old girl (not yet a woman) who moved from India to Ottawa, Ontario, to study at the prestigious University of Ottawa. I'm penning down my thoughts and beliefs to share my life experiences and lessons that come along with them that give a greater meaning to our existence and help us understand ourselves, others, and our lives better.

Moving from one country to another at eighteen wasn't as glamorous as I thought it would be. I learned that money played a significant role in the kind of lifestyle I wanted to sustain, and finances introduced mental, physical, and emotional challenges in my life. I had to embrace my solitude and be comfortable just on my own without needing a thing or anyone, before isolation became a "thing" with COVID-19 and everyone was forced to find a silver lining within their own premises. My familiarity with solitude allowed me to discover aspects of me as a human apart from my identity, gender, or race. This helped shed a new outlook on myself and the universal desires in each one of us.

Through the internet, I started discovering more people with the same ideologies and hurdles. It made me recognize the power of our stories and that we can share them to inspire and support each other through this maze of life.

Dealing with past events that have become my present-day insecurities (which penetrate my anxiety of the future) is what made me re-evaluate two things. What am I doing on this planet? And who, exactly, am I? In other words, "why are we here when ultimately everyone has to create their own happiness?" is the ever-daunting question on my mind. I learned that this question often consumes everyone's mind at some point in their journey, along with, why are people suffering? What does it mean to love and be loved? Is there a God? How can I be rich? And most important of them all, what is the purpose for my existence on this planet? These are some of the questions I attempt to address in this book. Exploring each one helped me get to know myself and empathize with those around me.

Many people are good at giving advice and suggesting to others how they should live, but some lack the ability to apply those measures to their own lives. People say things like, "Be grateful," but what does it truly mean to be grateful toward life? How do we get into a frequency of feeling good at all times? How do we identify whether our thoughts are selfish or maligned?

The reason I decided to write this book was to share the power of our minds. The following epiphanies helped me overcome the challenges of my life, so I could enjoy it and live my best self in contentment.

I believe in the power of perspective because it has helped me see the beauty of my, and everyone else's, existence. I don't emphasize what that means in a tangible world, but it helps me be in complete awe of my life and makes me realize that how we wire ourselves on the inside is eventually what manifests on the outside. Whenever I reminisce, the past seems beautiful, the present seems abundant, and the future seems hopeful.

Everything in this world is truly a team effort and respecting every existence we encounter is truly an opportunity to reflect who we are. We all are in this together and without the help of everyone in my life, it wouldn't even have been possible to write this book!

I am now more self-aware, which has helped me control my emotions in order to feel good and see the silver linings in my life. I have seen myself evolve through finding inner contentment, valuing love and abundance, and recognizing a stronger belief in myself. I never thought that I could be the person who is simply happy. In reality, it's the little things we think are insignificant that hold the most power in our life.

Through books, family, and others, I learned that not everyone is born with a perfect method of living life, but we all must learn how to make it the best we can. This book attempts to free you from yourself. Reading this book might not change your perspective, but it's a good distraction and escape from everyday life. Reading also stimulates the mind; it's like a gym for your brain. You might sweat like a pig, but the results are phenomenal.

Others can only guide us toward the direction where the light is coming from, but it is our responsibility to walk the path to enlightenment. We get to choose what our mind inhales or exhales, and this determines the life we create for ourselves. No two people have the same fingerprint, so everyone will have different challenges. However, some basic attitude rewiring can help us unlock jammed, closed, or unknown doors within ourselves.

If you are truly willing to make an impactful change within yourself that will help you live with a smile on your face, then please leave your prejudices, cynicism, and stubbornness outside. I welcome you to put on your reading and self-introspective lenses.

Chapter One

The Past

"We suffer not from the events in our lives but from our judgement about them." —Epictetus

Appreciating Our Past

When our lives feel out of control, we tend to delve into our past to find a scapegoat. We search for faults in our genes, parents, family, friends, and even God to make sense of why we are who we are. We search for faults so much that we end up limiting the paradigms that we base our outlook and understanding of our life upon and other times, we rewind the past like a broken record in our minds that forms deep knots of regret within us. We bring individuals from our memory bank to the forefront who made a significant dent in our lives at some point and make them eminently relevant in today's very moment, undermining the fact that they somewhere helped to steer the wheel of our life to Now. In an instant, this moment we are breathing will become the past, and what seems uncontrollable is actually very controllable right in this moment. The past is a stardust of our present selves, and it will be always unique to us and that is our secret superpower.

While it is okay to delve into the past in the moments of despair, happiness, or simply boredom, it is imperative to understand that constantly pondering something that does not exist clouds our ability to be fully present in the moment. Blaming all our psychological and emotional issues on unfortunate events that occurred in the past causes us to overlook the current scenario. Obsessing over "what was" and "what if" scenarios can be utterly draining. It's like an eighth-grader studying grade five books and receiving an F(ail) as a result, then wondering why they are failing.

The past played a vital role in aging and evolving us to this very moment. It's important to note the underlying themes or challenges that hit us the hardest and consider what we have done about them. Have we succumbed and become bitter, or did we learn and grow from our experiences? And, till the time we don't move forward with grace and unlock a greater art within us of detachment, it will always remain a part of us as baggage.

Seek Forgiveness

It all starts from understanding ourselves from the day we were born. Sometimes, things that we currently ache for in this life are determined by where we left off in a past life. Whenever a person dies, it feels like some energy that was running their life simply left their vessel and that very energy that entered at the time of birth comes from somewhere like the fuel in our cars or current for the electricity. In a way, you can call it reincarnation. Our soul carefully chose what it was supposed to experience in its time on this earth. Our soul chose this planet to exist in human form. We did not choose the time and date we were born—an entity called "the soul" harvested it. With the alignment of the stars in the sky at the moment of birth, the soul selects its biological parents and that is our primal life's map. Have you ever met someone with whom you feel a connection from a past life? The question isn't why the soul chose this life or identity, but the answer is that it did, and that is what we have been given to live with. If we do not even readily engage ourselves wholesomely in the present, then we can neither figure out the past nor even remotely decipher the reason for our existence to ourselves.

People go through some really difficult times and some of those times have an everlasting impact. When we ask the question "why me?" then we must also keep in mind, this is the same question that many are asking around the globe. We are born with pre-requisites that we need to entertain as our challenges in our present life. If the past life karmas weren't a real phenomenon, then all of us would have the same struggles and not the ones that are specifically designed and unique to us in given circumstances. We endure our unknown mistakes and that is a true punishment because we don't even know what we are being held accountable for. The universe that created us is our true parent, and one of many amazing qualities about parents is that they forgive their child when the child is sincerely remorseful and apologetic about their actions and behaviours. Similarly, we don't have a clue about why we inherit the adversities or pain-stricken circumstances, but if we begin and end our day earnestly seeking and asking for forgiveness for whatever wrong we may unknowingly have committed and to also give strength to the ones we are seeking forgiveness from, to move on and forgive, the universe has a way of forgiving and easing our repentances. Even criminals who are incarcerated for a crime are pardoned sooner than their sentence when they exhibit good behaviours and attitude.

Although a mind's cognitive abilities develop over time with experiences and life-education, we always have our inner voice telling us to engage in actions or words that unburden us. It tells us to choose a mindset that makes us happy or to select the action that will lead us to inner liberation. It will always be a juxtaposition to what we are feeling in that very moment. Something inside us is always indicating that we should have a mind of our own that is fertilized with hope and optimism instead of limiting ourselves based on previous experiences and that voice is at times subdued by our ignorance.

That contradiction makes us look for enlightenment, especially in moments when we are hurt. That is the beauty of falling down; it is an opportunity to kiss the ground on which we firmly stand tall, so we can feel and appreciate the power of gravity and pick ourselves back up. Because of our inner contradiction, we seldom choose to ignore our inner voice that aches for love and peace. We distance ourselves from achieving serenity: a tune or rhythm that makes us want to dance to the sound of life. The gap of growth between the past and present is beautiful because our musings help us identify and attempt to resolve our deepest existential questions.

Analyzing Traumatic Events

As humans, we all desire to be appreciated and loved. However, every single human on this planet has experienced traumatic events, usually in childhood. These could be (but are not limited to) being beaten by parents, losing grandparents, scarcity in basic needs, witnessing separation, and other tragedies. We all endure some experience that impacts us so deeply that it scars or imprints on our minds forever.

If you're reading this and have lived comfortably, it's important to empathize with those less fortunate.

Some children are born in a refugee camp without any biological parents or commercial goods stores around. Others are born into a family with a history of drug abuse due to an atrocious environment influenced by poverty. The worst cases can result in children being sent to foster homes. In India, where I was raised, some children are outcast at birth by default due to their parents' socio-economic circumstances and grow up in slums, neglected. The condition of their lives invites slavery and abuse upon them. We can only imagine what it's like to exist in those kids' shoes, and it's difficult to face the tragedy that some people face from the day they were born.

Looking back, there may have been times our parents could not fulfill our desires because they did not have the means to do so. They might have been hard at work to put food on our table and send us to school while keeping us alive and away from evil. Not to mention, they were likely working through their own challenges. During these times, some of us grew up insecure because of how these limitations caused kids to make fun of us for how we looked or what we did not have access to.

Luckily, it is possible to recognize the challenges that inhibited us from being comfortable within our own skin. Many people do not even get a moment to pause or receive competent guidance to encourage an analysis of the pain they are trying to shove under the mud, but in our present world, run by the internet, we have a choice to seek help. In today's world of social media, even beautiful people are not spared. Everyone is judged through filters or Photoshop, so much so that the reality is lost. We are all distancing ourselves from the reality of life. Even focusing on the unreal clouds our perception of reality. No matter what, we all are dealing with fitting in and even the people we want to fit in with are subconsciously battling this dilemma.

In a way, we are fighting a battle that was imposed upon us from the moment we came into existence. We all have to fight this battle with the tools we are born with. The struggle varies between mental, physical, or both and we need to find new weapons within us, so we can rise like a phoenix from the ashes every morning we wake up.

Growing up, I gave too much attention to the people who ruined my innocence; high school teens are some of the biggest devils (and morons) in the world. Some people I loved dearly, like my friends or a crush, would make up stories about my moral character and call me horrific names, some of which I didn't even know the meaning of! To remove that stigma, I would pretend to be like others or pretend to be free-spirited, party-loving, or some cool socialite trying to fit in amongst the older and cooler kids which resulted in my parents physically disciplining me (which still echoes in my brain as one of the worst things parents can do). Sure, I was being dumb, and my parents were trying to control me when I was trying to find myself. But in those moments, I used to despise my parents so much that I just wanted to run away from home.

Years later, I now realize why my parents were so controlling. It's because they knew the kind of people who exist in our society, and they did not want their child to be stripped of any divinity by coming in contact with pollutants that deviate one from good habits. I could have chosen to despise my parents or close friends after all those years but empathizing with their mindset made it easier for me to understand why something happened the way it did.

We all move forward in life with the ones that hurt us. They can be our best friends, our extended family, or even our siblings. Their presence in our current lives reminds us of their actions that might have rubbed us the wrong way at some point in the past. So, do we just tag them as villains our entire life? No, we do not. We try to be uncalled-for heroes by bottling up things inside and not realizing the only thing that ages better with time inside a bottle is wine. If someone or something the other person has done that caused you strife, then it's your job to find a way to communicate your feelings to the other person or share with a confidant to iron out and dispose of the negativity because it does not serve any good to anyone holding on to it.

Everyone deserves forgiveness, empathy, and a second chance. We not only move forward in time, but we must also move forward in our minds. Understanding why someone did what they did isn't letting them get away with it guilt-free. It can spark a strength within us that says, you were okay, you are okay, and you will be okay, no matter what. Empathy is a spark that pushes us to do something for ourselves that will ultimately make us happy. It's an awakening not to do something similar to others. Imagine how much of a delight you will be for others to be around!

If people with evil intentions were aware of what they were doing and the outcome it would bring back upon them, they probably wouldn't do it. That fact applies to us as well. We have lived through those experiences because, at some point, we invited those people into our lives. The universe is merely serving us the dish that we picked the ingredients for in some known or unknown circumstance. Everything negative that may have happened in our life certainly won't go away if we are holding on to it tightly. However, we can find some closure by treating any bitter experience as a form of repentance that our soul led us through with grace.

Acceptance of Ourselves

We all genuinely want to accept who, what, and how we are. It's our aim to be undefined by the things that surround us. We should not derive our self-worth based on how much we own or what others think of us. That would only add to the likelihood of being misjudged by other people's perceptions and opinions. We all want acceptance, which starts with accepting ourselves first. But we cannot get there if we don't calm the drums that beat within us. Everything in the past will keep haunting us if we let it and do not recognize why something is holding us back.

To accept ourselves, we must first accept each being, every moment, every circumstance and every experience that we have endured. We cannot impose what we feel or how we are on others, and they cannot understand what we feel, and that expectation is inconsequential; we must try our best to coexist and that only comes with the acceptance of others and being responsible for one's attitude in any kind of relationship. We do not and cannot control what everyone else does or says, and that should not justify our own behaviour. To accept the flaws of others is to attain maturity of the fact that everyone's on their own journey. Each person has their own understanding of the world, driven by their specific experiences. We shouldn't just accept the flaws of others, but we must also accept the good in others and encourage it with every chance we get. If we keep magnifying the weaknesses of others either to ourselves or them, then that is all we will keep interacting with and the same goes for us.

"Beauty is in the eyes of the beholder."
—Margaret Wolfe Hungerford, Molly Bawn, 1878

Pobody's Nerfect

We should encourage the goodness in others to take over their own selves. No person is entirely bad or entirely good, and that is applicable to us too. We aren't entirely bad or good, we are a hybrid of both aspects, and we must always fuel the goodness in us to triumph over the not-so-good.

Your past experiences formed you into the person who wants to pick up this book and read it. Your history made you a person who wants to move forward and look ahead. It made you hopeful, it made you believe in yourself, and it shaped your likes and dislikes. Your past was the road you travelled to be here. Every road has speed bumps, stop signs, and detours. It could have been worse, but it wasn't.

Scrap your idea of a perfect life; it does not exist! Plus, it'd be boring. Growing up, I used to spend a lot of my holidays with my paternal aunt. She is a very spiritual person who, at the time, was going through major setbacks and struggles in her life. As a widowed mom of three young kids who earned a below-minimum-wage salary as a teacher, she still found time and kindness to educate me about the inner self, God, the power of prayer, and how to be a class act. She taught me to pray whenever I was feeling ill and pray to angels to help me during my exams. She opened me up to the power of affirmations and how to spend my time saying good things instead of fixating on a negative situation. She could have been bogged down by life, but she actively chose to stay in high spirits.

Years later, when I was in Canada, I called her and told her I was very thankful for the knowledge she imparted in me because they came in handy when

I was by myself. Those learnings helped me become a believer in magic and gave me hope. On that call, she advised that I must do the same for others if I was truly grateful and sincere about my feelings toward her. What a wonderful thought! Being grateful to someone isn't just saying thank you to them but also imbibing and spreading their goodness. Although she now lives miles away from me, I'll forever have her in my heart because of the priceless gifts of strength that she imparted in me.

The absence of our loved ones is the greatest reminder that nothing lasts forever. We must celebrate the love they made us feel. If we truly love and are grateful for the love we felt, we must spread the love instead of expecting others to replace it. It's similar to when we earn money. We must spend it to realize its utility; it's of no use to us if we are just storing it in the bank. The things we have learned from our mentors aren't fully absorbed until we share the love and knowledge with others. We are not born perfect but along our journey, we meet people whose goodness makes us reflect on the goodness that we can sharpen within and inspire others. Many people are also going to find us imperfect and flawed and that is completely okay. Not everyone will like us for who we are because they are seeing us through their lenses and making peace with that fact will save us from unnecessary insecurities. Accepting others disliking you is an art of the evolved. No matter what you will do to please others, it will never be enough, and it is not your responsibility either. It is their responsibility to manage their perception, so save yourself the time and let them figure it out.

The Power of Imagination

"Everything you can imagine is real." —Pablo Picasso

When I was a teenager, my father never allowed me to go out of the house after 7:00 p.m. In exchange, he bought me a portable red coloured MP3 player that I used to take to the terrace with me. I'd gaze at the stars while listening to hip hop and R&B music, visualizing what I wanted in my life as a budding teen. Back in 2006, an MP3 player was a super cool gadget to own, but I still despised my father and hated him for controlling me, overlooking how he bought me everything with his hard-earned money to keep me entertained at home and I did absolutely everything I could to rebel against him.

Due to his constrictions on my life, my rebellion was primarily imaginative. I visualized everything that I could not own as a twelve to thirteen-year-old in real life. I imagined owning a cell phone, a car, all the high-quality attire I could desire, and all the chips and junk food that I could possibly eat. I envisioned living alone and having no one, not even my parents, around to nag me. I used that time with my MP3 player to imagine every possible thing a teenager would want. Eventually, my parent's respective careers started doing well and my visualizations started to manifest. I had a cellphone at the age of thirteen. Then, I moved to a different country at the age of eighteen, where I had the ability to buy and eat whatever I wanted. Moving to a new country was like a restart to my life. I met new people from different backgrounds who just wanted to have fun and enjoy their lives the best they could, irrespective of their financial status. The societies and lifestyles in Western countries are more inclined toward individualistic existence rather than the collective. It was liberating because no one knew me or cared how much money my family had, and I could decide who I wanted to hang out and associate with and that was everything that I had imagined as a teenage girl on my rooftop with music blasting in my ears.

After my imagination manifested and I moved far away for university, I just did not have my parents who, up to that point, would do anything to keep me safe and fed. I became my own parent and my guardian. I was surprisingly prepared after spending all my time gazing at the sky with Lil Wayne blasting in my ears, reflecting upon the things that would bring me happiness. Looking back, I am grateful to my parents for being strict. By not letting me go to sleepovers, they pretty much killed my social life, which allowed me to focus on myself. It opened up a beautiful world in my imagination where I was discovering who I really am and who I wanted to be. I sought divine magic to liberate and surround me with open-minded people from all walks of life who just wanted to have a good time in life and not mentally assassinate each other. I imagined and prayed, and these valuable skills could have only come from being on my own. Even though I did not have much practical exposure in life, I got all the exposure to North American culture through movies, music, and television.

I learned the power of imagination, meditation, God, solitude, and the primal fact of life that I am the creator of my own happiness, and my mind is the dictator of it. It is difficult to grasp in that moment, but eventually, years later, when I spent time with myself, it did. Our imagination is a vehicle that takes us to places we truly want to go and gives birth to our ultimate desired self. It gives us space to desire all that we want to have and be in this human form. When we imagine, we subconsciously create our reality that manifests in the tangible world as ideas, opportunities, and circumstances. We so badly wish for another world at times, a perfect world. We might not be able to realize that in the moment, the environment we are currently in is exactly what we need to build the life we ache for.

While we are growing up, our families are growing up with us too. Our parents, siblings, and friends are evolving with us. We are learning each day and so is everyone else. Somehow, our tolerance reduces when it comes to others; we expect everyone to behave appropriately and perfectly. We must not constantly play the redundant blame game.

Shedding the Old

You can choose right now to accept your past as a way of blessing or choose to live in your mental hell. Either way, it's you who has to live with what you are sowing in your subconscious. You are the one who will attract unpleasant experiences over and over again. Whenever I looked back at my past, I only remembered people who bullied me or my parents scolding me and not buying me things like other parents did. I recalled struggling in extreme winter while carrying groceries in cheap boots, uphill in -30C weather, and often going through anxiety and panic attacks due to financial and emotional uncertainties. I had no idea that getting an education could be so torturous to one's mental and physical health. When I started to switch my outlook in my late twenties, I realized I had some amazing friends who I cherished and were there for me because it was really lonely in a new country. I started admiring my parents for working hard so they could send me to a prestigious school and that realization came after I started working part-time jobs in Canada as general help at a food court or as a gardener who plucked weeds from people's backyards to support my expenses in university. Whether the glass is half-empty or half-full is simply an outlook. Fill your glass back up, find an outlook and stick to it; don't be a human seesaw.

Each day the clock is ticking, the sun is shining, the birds are chirping—even nature has accepted the order of cosmos. With the acceptance of the laws of nature, the world moves forward. Whatever happened, happened. The only way out of the loop is to move forward and keep doing what fulfills your needs of the current hour. Slowing down because of the hooks that pull us back will only slow down the pace with which we move forward. Every second we waste being a victim or allowing anything to have a hold over us, we aren't living our life. We are living what outside forces dictate for us. The jobs that I did as a student, I could never do in India because of what my peers would think of me, and I am so glad that I got an opportunity to work at laborious jobs since they kept me active, engaged, and taught me a thing or two about self-sustaining errands while supporting myself financially. At that time, it felt like a tiring struggle with no hopes of living a decent life, but that is exactly what I needed to do to earn a decent living. It also gave me a newfound appreciation and respect for everyone trying to put food on their family's table with their hard work.

Acceptance of the very fact that we are not alone, and our past comes with challenges no matter what, allows us to set expectations of our life and ourselves. Acceptance of our past will enable us to accept the history of others. Whatever it may have been, the beauty of it led you to this very moment.

There are a few basic generic and universal facts we must accept about life:

- We all have the same fate—the death of our human form.

- We all make mistakes, and mistakes are an opportunity to introspect.
- We all are similar and different at the same time.
- No one can be exactly like us, or the world would be pretty darn boring.
- We all change like the seasons.
- All of us want to be liked and accepted for who we are.
- All of us have regrets and baggage.
- The earth revolves around that big yellow thing in the sky.
- And believe it or not, every relationship is temporary.

Moving On . . .

It's essential to revisit the pains our soul wanted us to learn something from. When we introspect and analyze what serves us and what does not, we discover the underlying truth that nothing lasts forever. We can only control what we choose to play in our minds. Our past had influential events that wanted us to change somehow, and if we are not prepared to learn from our past, we can never move forward and grow. We will always be trapped by limited thoughts about a situation that causes us to experience the same frustrations. Our past was a lesson that we needed to learn in order to tackle what is to come.

If the mind is not occupied, then time will repeat those incidences in our mind over and over again to the point that it will continue manifesting itself. Our mind is a puppy; it needs constant feeding, training, and distraction. We overthink the past because we might not be using our time in the present moment wisely. We should do things that can engage us, like cleaning the clutter around us, going for a walk, or uplifting people instead of finding prey upon which to blame our life's problems or focusing on finding faults in others.

Sometimes our baggage unknowingly dictates our behaviours, and our behaviour ultimately dictates our relationships and lives. It's important to talk through unpleasant experiences to give them closure and accept your new reality. Reflecting with objectivity and acceptance while avoiding a victim mentality can illuminate answers from within and even inform strategies to cope with it. Most of our negative emotions—anger, pessimism, cynicism, and anxiety— are an outcome of how much peace we have made with our past and what habits we have accustomed ourselves to.

Habits are not taught; they are learned. If we have made a habit of reacting negatively to situations, then every situation will present faults. As humans, we unknowingly seek those faults as we get comfortable with our jobs, our bodies, and even our dressing style. No day is the same, like no joke is funnier the second time around. Even our body weight and temperature are not consistent, so how can our limitations be so aggressively engrained? Why do we react to life with a constant state of worry, self-victimization, or a defensive mentality? We may understand that every day is different yet we are half-minded about the role that we play in each new day.

We have two important aspects of ourselves: internal and external, or inner and outer state of being. Yes, our minds are wild and powerful, and dictate what happens in our lives and how much we control it. Even though it resides in our body, it's the hardest thing to take care of and control. Our breath is inhaled and exhaled to complete one cycle of breathing. Similarly, we need to balance our external and internal reality to complete our cycle of mental stimulation. Sometimes, our mind plays tricks on us and makes us feel grey, but if we externally and physically push those thoughts away by simply participating in some activity, we can make way for new thoughts to take their place. Ideally, they should be thoughts of love and fulfillment. When we use our strength to better ourselves, even the cosmos helps us to get there.

Live in the Moment

To live in the present is to see what we have and what we can do with it. The ultimate way of controlling one's mind is not to lurk in the past or anticipate the future, but to simply look around and witness the moment. Take a deep breath and put on a smile. The person who can master the art of living in the present is truly enlightened.

Our body can never rewind its aging; no anti-aging cream can re-create innocence back on the face. Whether you like it or not, a body is aging along with its natural clock. That biological clock moves to align us with the forces of nature. Our mind, the only thing we control in our lives, is waiting for us to catch up so it can live at its full potential.

Sometimes, the quickest way to do that is to laugh and change the flow of energy in our bodies. Laughter is a nudge to be present in the moment and be accepting of it too. Laughter is a must! If you can't look back without laughing at life, then you haven't truly moved on. Some way or the other, the same experiences will recycle. One moment of delving into the past with bravery and ownership can zap our minds to cut the mental attachments to it. We can accept the reality that no longer exists and focus on what will make us feel good in this very moment.

I used to look back at some cringe-worthy moments in my life, like calling a girl fat or friending random people on Facebook to appear cool. I am in no way proud of those actions, but it's just a reminder that I am not perfect, and neither is anyone else. We need to let go and accept that we are all truly flawed. That is where the beauty of life lies. We push each other to be our best selves; we are each other's motivation. Other people can be the fire that we need to light up our passions, but that is only if it's comprehended that way.

Some awful things happen to really good people, and no one knows why. When I look at the atrocities around the world, I pray and hope for some divine intervention. I hope for the prosperity of all, but unpleasant things still happen. We must give ourselves love to move forward, whether by working out, eating well, relaxing, or remaining calm and hopeful. It's not fair to blame God for atrocities around the world; God didn't do it. We did it to each other, either for greed or pride. However, we have the power to make it better by helping someone in need or accepting others for whom they are.

When we spend time with ourselves, it helps us understand ourselves. Our past is only a means to improve something that is lacking in us. If we do not learn what we were supposed to, the past will always remain a part of our present. Only when regretting is replaced with ownership will the past begin to make sense. No one else will feel the pain or hurt we feel; no one can help us but ourselves.

Isaac Newton discovered gravity by observing an apple falling on the ground from the tree. He stated that everything was getting pulled by the earth by its magnetic force called gravity. The curious mind of Albert Einstein wasn't satisfied with that explanation of gravity. He questioned that if everything is getting pulled by the earth, why is everything not hugging the ground and how is earth able to float in space? And why are trees still able to stand tall? With research, comparison, and asking the right questions, he discovered that gravity is a result of curved space (emptiness in our universe) and time due to mass and energy in the space of our universe. It's not as simple as a magnetic force pulling everything toward itself. It's up to us to not settle with an uneasy or vague explanation of something; it does not lead to closure. Only a positive and forward-moving mindset brings an ultimate and satisfying conclusion.

Reminiscing

Every challenge is a wonderful opportunity to mature and understand life a bit better. Asking ourselves pertinent questions can lead to great discoveries within. Instead of merely admitting and believing that we were unlucky, let's ask ourselves what challenges we can discover within us then seek ways to overcome them.

If we want to fill a bucket of water from a well but we only show up with a bowl, we ought to be disappointed when we either don't have enough water or spend hours collecting the amount of water we need. Whenever we look back, we need to be open-minded and feel comfortable pointing a finger at ourselves when we didn't allow our higher self to guide us in the moment. Only when we recognize that we have also dropped the ball in a situation by acting with a negative belief and outlook, will we ever be able to admit the fact that we acted hastily and attempt to change.

When I was a teenager, people made fun of me for the way I looked and that my family wasn't as wealthy as theirs. I was made to feel inferior because of my lack of friends or the place I lived; basically, people searched for reasons to make me feel inferior. At times, I even made-up stories to frame my character as a promiscuous girl to appear cool and to distract from people's teasing. Of course, that made things even worse. I remember a girl from my class wrote crap about me on her Facebook wall. I had never even spoken to or hung out with her! Sometimes, my friend and I would sit in one corner of the classroom, and everyone else would sit together away from us. It was as if we were hyenas, and they were a pack of wolves. (Little did I know, hyenas can be even more powerful than lions, so I'm giving myself a compliment.) Every time I thought of my hometown and the acquaintances I met there, it filled me with anxiety.

Years later, those same girls who rejected me, reached out to let me know how they regretted being unkind to me. They explained that they just wanted to belong and had jumped on the bandwagon that was making me a target for everyone to blame. I look back and wonder, what did I do to make myself that target? The answer dawned that I did not try to be who they wanted me to be. Instead, I stayed in my own dreamy world, which helped me grow and see the possibilities of life that no one else could. It led me to take a risk and move out of the country to explore a different world and meet different people. Those people helped me find my path away from toxicity. The fact that I can truly thank people from my past and that they hold no relevance in my life is a win in itself.

People are going to find reasons to dislike you, no matter what. They will say belittling things to your face and behind your back if they are not getting their desired result. Along the way, many people will pull you down so they can feel better about themselves. At that moment, it hurts, and it feels like we do not fit in this world. But remember to immunize yourself from the infections that others want you to catch, and in time, with patience, it will pay off. Instead of playing the games of other people, focus on building yourself.

All that nonsense led me to be a sensitive person who does not judge people based on their material possessions or comment on what others are doing or not doing. I often see this sensitivity missing from people. People judge others based on their outfits or the house they live in, not knowing that a person who is not dressed well might be a labourer at a farm that produces tomatoes for their meals. It's a wonderful thing to be sensitive and only impart upon others what you would like to be done to you. When we are sensitive and aware, compassion builds, and we automatically attract sensible people. Lack of people's acceptance made me want to sharpen the good qualities within me. Sensitivity is a superpower; it means to use your senses. Whenever you shed light on an event, your sensibilities will allow you to improve yourself.

Everything that happened in the past was exactly how it was meant to be. However, it's easier for our minds to focus on the bad instead of the good. Whenever we look back and focus on all the challenges that made us more resilient and wiser, we can find solace that they helped prepare us for this very moment. It becomes second nature to look back and simply be happy with everything that occurred. Every person who crossed our path did so to teach us something. All the regrets vanish, the bad sensations iron themselves out, and life does not remain a mystery anymore. Our history helped us become closer to our soul and allowed us to discover our own power that we should wear as a badge of honour.

Chapter Two

Happiness

"Success is getting what you want, happiness is wanting what you get." —W.P. Kinsella

Happiness is the most under-explained word in our vocabulary. Think about it for a second; what does it mean to be happy? Is it an uplifting emotion? Is it temporary? Or is it just the feeling that follows a pleasant event like winning the lottery? We identify happiness as the result of our desires being fulfilled but rarely does one truly feel it. How often are we sincerely present in the moment when our desires are being fulfilled? Usually, the blessings are taken for granted, and the feeling of gratitude becomes one of greed and expectations. We sabotage our blessings when we get too comfortable with feelings of unhappiness.

When someone is looking for a job, they're seeking an entrance into a company. When one works at an entry-level position for years, they complain about not getting ahead in that company. Even in so-called happy moments, other challenges of life continually present themselves. It's an endless cycle of things pulling us up and pushing us down.

Recognize Reality

If an event can easily cause you to feel angry or happy, then you are easily manipulated. We believe that we can't be easily manipulated or influenced because we are well-educated, experienced, or feel aware of these forces. However, it is with this mindset that we are probably the most vulnerable to getting orchestrated. Like most people, I also scrolled social media every second that I could. At times, in my dreams, insignificant details that I had come across or people would pop up who I did not even know personally, made me realize that I was filling my mind with unnecessary people and details. Those, in a way, laid out expectations of myself whether I admitted it or not. We form subconscious mental bonds with the people who follow on social media platforms, which makes us want to keep peeking at their lives for the addiction of entertainment. Why do we want to post a picture from our birthday party on social media? Because we had seen someone else do it, which in a way compelled us to show the rainbows in our lives as well. This is one example of how we, at times, are unknowingly being held captive in the prison of manipulation. Why do we need to know information about other people's lives? It is like being at an uninvited party only to eavesdrop. The little acts of distraction further us from ourselves unknowingly, day by day. They loosen our ability to focus, be present in the moment, develop self-preserving habits, and be wholly aware of ourselves. Life is truly too short to waste on the unnecessary.

The idea that we "know it all" blocks our simplicity and makes us want an immediate answer to everything. If you can't create happiness within your ability and in simplicity, then you are always searching for external forces to create that emotion or give you that high.

The value we place on events or things is directly proportionate to how happy they make us. If our happiness is contingent on worldly things, then while we feel good about owning them, they can never bring us lasting contentment. Rather, they create a contrary emotion of greed or needing validation. This is because we haven't tuned our mind to be satisfied with a temporary fulfillment of our needs. Instead, we continuously chase the feeling of needing more. The idea that the more we have, the happier we will be isn't entirely logical. It's like assuming that multiple dishes on our table will pacify our hunger more.

Being happy as a result of an event (like receiving a nice sweater as a surprise gift) makes it easier to react to events with a different extreme emotion like anger.

When someone pisses us off, we get upset and angry over that event. So why do we need to be dependent on an event to make us feel an extreme emotion of our perceived happiness?

It is not the things that make us happy. It is the value we place on them. Not to say that we do not need utensils to complement our lives, but we mustn't substitute our needs with our wants.

Attitude of Gratitude

Most of us take so many things for granted, such as being able to breathe, move a limb, sleep, wake up, see, hear, and eat. We get so accustomed to looking to things outside of ourselves to satisfy us that we overlook the priceless things we have already been given. These necessities are invaluable and form essential elements of our lives. Without any of them, life is inherently more difficult. We must always give these blessings acknowledgement, and anything more than our basic needs is a cherry on the cake.

Happiness is the atmosphere in our minds. It is the climate one lives in within oneself. If we are replacing what really matters with how blessed we already are, then an atmosphere of happiness will always be present in our world. Do we ever thank our body for producing blood, iron, calcium, and protein, which are all necessary for being alive? We don't; we are not even aware of how much we already owe to our lives for sustaining our human selves. How often do we say thank you before having a meal? Or relay gratitude after being hugged by a loved one? We only focus on what should cover our body or which brand to represent ourselves with to be accepted by others. We focus on the house we live in, not the home that we already have: our soul. We do not even value the biological relationships that we inherit; instead, we give our best to others.

The more we focus on what's outside of us, the emptier we will become on the inside. Eventually, we will have no other choice but to focus on what is inside of us. We feel connected to the world by interacting through the screens of our electronic devices, but we've become so disconnected from the people who exist around us. We focus on our scarcity while desiring abundance. How is that in synchronicity? We are so out of sync between how we feel inside and what we manifest on the outside. We tend to take for granted things like opening a tap to fill a glass with water that quenches our thirst and sleeping on a comfortable bed.

We define value based on the cars we drive or the homes we live in. Let's hypothetically assume that we are all billionaires. What mouth would we eat the food with if we were all billionaires? The same mouth. Which body would we dress up with nicer clothes? The same body. Are you hoping to get a mind or soul transplant when you are a billionaire? NEWS FLASH: the science isn't there yet. Some basic necessities that we all need remain the same throughout the world.

By focusing on what appears ordinary or "lacking," we create space for emptiness. This attitude makes us look for other things to fill the void that make us feel good on a deeper level. If we let our basic blessings become our primary fuel of happiness, everything will be an adventure that we will happily undertake. Ultimately, we create the background in which we are acting in this theatre of life. It is up to us to give meaning to what happiness means to us, whether we want to make it a permanent or temporary emotion for ourselves. Anything outside of us will always be temporary, and everything within us will be ours to keep forever.

The Other Half

Love, the most beautiful feeling that exists, is another reason people find to feel unhappy or incomplete. Some people aren't happy when they are with someone, but also aren't happy when they are single. When I was single, all I wanted was to be paired up with a nice mate. However, some of the best things of life are enjoyed when single (like music, which truly strings the chords of the soul). Wine tastes better, the ability to focus on self-improvement is stronger, and one can feel more connected to God (if one is are lucky). The only bad part about being single is sometimes feeling like a third wheel when spending time with a couple, especially during their honeymoon period.

Being single opens the doors for us to pack our bags and go anywhere in the world, anytime we wish to. It gives us the chance to take over the whole bed, fart shamelessly, eat without being judged, and sleep past noon without being called lazy! Of course, I understand we all want to belong; we want to belong to a country, a city, an area, a family, a religion, or a culture. Often, most importantly, we want to belong to someone.

The idea of love is embellished even more when one is single. We feel incomplete as a person and want another person to come and complete our lives. In reality, we don't have to be paired up with someone to feel those emotions. We humans have so many other types of relationships that make us feel loved and wanted—such as siblings, friends, family, co-workers, everyday acquaintances, and of course, the best of them all, a dog—but we place a huge amount of weight on our romantic relationships.

I was single for a very long time, and at the beginning of my twenties, I used to feel desperate about finding someone to be with. I surely and thankfully quickly realized that it was so difficult to find someone who gets and understands me, and no checklist of attributes will ever match up to that. I used to spend my days waking up super early to exercise and get to work before everyone else. I'd eat proper and healthy meals and by the time evening kicked in, Billie Holiday's "(In My) Solitude" would become my jam with a glass of wine. Solitude is like bitter gourd, it is bitter at first, but the health benefits are numerous. When we are around other people, we unknowingly get influenced. We have to abide by certain social expectations, and we also deliberately try to fit in. We engage in unnecessary conversations and conflicts that further deviate us from who we truly are, it is limiting. Being by oneself is beautiful because it allows us to know ourselves, be who we truly are and expand our thoughts and ideas. Solitude allows us to discover ourselves, prioritize our needs, and attain personal growth by addressing conflicts within. It is really a way to feel our existence through our soul and mind whereas constantly being around people drains us of the ability to internalize, imagine, and evolve! It is a gift from universe to be able to live with oneself. Many people cannot even be by themselves because they get bored by themselves. If they cannot be by themselves, they wouldn't even be interesting to be around. When one isn't even appreciative of their own life, they will never be appreciative of others time either. Isolation and solitude are necessary tools that are required to develop as a human being and feel those breaths that we have been given. It helps us to become self-aware and also indulge in activities that brings us joy, ignite our passions, and simply love who we are.

In the beginning, it was difficult not to have love, family, or a man in my day-to-day life and especially after unsuccessful attempts at relationships, I had to step back from dating and re-evaluate my idea of love. After days of contemplation with easy come and easy go friends, books, and lying around to wait for a miracle, I started enjoying my drink, music, yoga, cooking, reading a book, lighting a candle, and sleeping in the middle of the bed with hairy legs. I accepted that I am my own partner-in-crime who is in a relationship with myself. I no longer felt the void of another person and I started holding myself tight on the inside. I felt complete by living in the moment and witnessing what I am supposed to. If someone does come along, they will just join my journey instead of me waiting for that person as my life passes by.

Being by myself made me realize that we do inherently crave some kind of companionship. Since that wasn't available, I searched for a divine connection. When I felt that my soul ultimately craves enlightenment (truest freedom), an understanding of this maze called life, self-improvement, and a stronger relationship with myself, my soul became my mate. Being single is an excellent time to grow your interests in new hobbies, be a good friend, and develop who you really are in your innermost core. If you are single or in a troubled relationship, your soul wants you to connect with it and grow as a person. Once you fill the void within yourself, you won't feel the desperate need to couple up. When you are with someone, it is beautiful to have someone to grow old and share your life with, but if you become too needy and start imposing how you are on the other person, then that relationship is bound to cause sorrow.

Benefits of Loneliness

I moved at the age of eighteen to a country where I didn't know anyone, and I had to learn how to support myself financially. I did not realize that back in India, my parents had spoiled me with healthy meals and a cleaning lady to broom and mop the whole house. In Canada, the currency exchange at the time was fifty Indian rupees for one Canadian dollar so I was always very cautious and limited with my expenses. It took me a while to figure out how to live, do my own laundry, and cook my own meals, but slowly I got a grasp of it like many other immigrants worldwide. I called my parents for every single question about "how to life" and that brought me even closer to my parents. Our long-distance relationship made me understand how parenting is the most thankless job in the world and at times, kids simply become complacent toward their parents.

I lived in isolation for several years. Life was just about working, studying, sleeping, and keeping anxiety and depression at bay. I had no family members or a romantic partner to celebrate all the festivals, birthdays, or just simply share suppers with. I began to feel completely lonely and depressed, as though I had been forgotten by my creator and the world in which I existed.

With time, I started asking myself questions while listening to good tunes, such as what I could do to make myself happy because no one is looking out for me. I appreciated friends, acquaintances, and other people even more because they kept me going. Sometimes, simply being present in the moment, accepting, and living what we are supposed to live, or taking a few deep breaths can go a long way. And, of course, laughter is a must. It releases feel-good emotions in us that can bring hope and prevent getting stuck scrutinizing some nonsense in our heads.

At times I felt that I had no other choice or any energy to spare, so I'd curl up in my bed to watch TV and soon realized my life was just passing before me. At the end of the day, it hurt me, and it made me feel lonely, which affected my physical and mental health. In that boredom, I went back to imagining my self-goals. I couldn't wait for the perfect time when I'd be happy, so I decided to do things that would help me enjoy my life and feel a sense of purpose instead of being a sloth in my bed. I started cooking instead of eating take-out, I regularly cleaned and tidied my surroundings, or bought myself a coconut-milk-mint-chocolate-latte as a treat. Sometimes, I'd take a drive in my second-hand Cobalt that I purchased with money I'd saved from my less-than-exciting social life after my graduation. (No new outfits needed if you're not going out!)

While being alone doesn't seem as fun as being a part of social events, it can be, if we use the time to develop ourselves or do things that bring us joy. When I created an atmosphere of happiness while I was by myself, I always found the rainbows and sunshine in my world. Good souls always found me, whether in the form of a friend, a fellow immigrant neighbour, or even my landlords. When we pursue good for ourselves, angels appear in the form of an experience or physical disguise that helps us through rough times.

Contentment

When I started accepting where I was in my life and truly started seeing everything that I was blessed with instead of what I didn't have, I began to live in the moment. That is when I started feeling happy and content with who I was. I started realizing that I was exactly where I was supposed to be, and every challenge became a lesson to grow from because there was no other choice but to embrace life at that point and not have a ball of sadness internally because that is not fair to my temporary existence. The more I believed that I was adaptable and equipped to handle any scenario, the more comfortable and pleasant everything became. Happiness is nothing more than being content with what we have. Nothing changed externally but I just began to have more hopes for myself in the present moment.

Contentment brings happiness; happiness does not depend on anything or anyone outside of you. Ultimately, it's a power we generate within. Looking for more, or never being satisfied with what we have has been preached for far too long. It's a redundant and backward mindset. Contentment helps us see the things around us that we take for granted. It's generated within us by merely accepting what is and what is not.

Why do we fear creating happiness within ourselves? We feel that we shouldn't accept what our current circumstances are and that we always lack something or the other. The mindset that we need money, status, or success to have happiness is incomplete. Happiness is what creates abundance for us, not the other way around.

When you accept, you become content; when you become content, you feel satisfied; when you feel satisfied, you'll only create thoughts and vibrations that are positive. When you have positive thoughts and vibrations, you only attract positivity. When you attract positivity, you will have nothing to complain about, and everything will seem like a blessing. When you feel blessed and positive, your mind will make space for more thoughts that radiate your inner happiness. When your mind clears up, you will imagine things that will make you feel fulfilled. When you are able to imagine, you will infuse that in your DNA and get the push from within to do those things. When you can do what your clear mind really wants to do, then by default, you will be a happier person with yourself.

How can you give what you don't have? How do you expect others to be happy with you when you aren't happy with yourself? Happiness is a state of mind and being. It starts by accepting and being content as a result of our habits and frankly, it's not others' responsibility either.

Embracing the Circumstances

Acceptance is a very underrated virtue. It does not mean merely "to accept who you are." It also means accepting the situation that was and is, then from there building the steps for a staircase to a more acceptable life. When you appreciate what you have, you start seeing your old car and your small house as a blessing. When you are grateful in life, you only receive things that will further enhance your attitude of gratitude.

Accepting is giving recognition to what you have in your life and what you don't have. Gratitude comes from acceptance. Accept the vastness of this universe. Accept that it's not social media that connects us, but the air we breathe, the water we drink, and the food we eat. Did you know that the dust that blows from the Sahara Desert fertilizes our oceans for plankton on which marine life survives? The silent occurrences around us are a reason we exist together at the same time, and we are connected. Accept the job that you might not like but is paying your bills. Do that job to the best of your ability, so you can open doors for yourself to climb up. Accept difficult people instead of changing them because no one is going to change for you. It is deeper than that. It is what their soul chose for them. We are truly guiding each other to be our better selves.

We must accept our present circumstances because our past led us to where we are today. Our souls needed us to discover more about our strengths and shortcomings. If we always keep an open mind and look at a situation as a way to improve ourselves, then it will always be us who will come out as a winner.

When we are focused on others, we are not truly aligned with our reality and that is a waste of our own lives. Comparing our lives or lifestyles with others and creating emotions of jealousy is not only self-inflicted, unnecessary, and futile but also fogs our ability to count our blessings like mentioned before—being able to breathe, eat, sleep, work, laugh, and simply enjoying the priceless nature at free of cost! And if you don't embrace those blessings every living second, then you are forcing yourself to live a lie that profit-driven markets have sold you. Because in reality, every circumstance, no matter how perfect it may seem, has its own challenges. It is eventually up to us to overcome them. The subject isn't what is around; the subject is you and it is your own awareness of what matters the most.

Like we need to be told that we are loved and appreciated to feel good about our relationships or work; similarly, everything that serves and supports our life also needs recognition and it develops as second nature with everyday practice. Our body cannot survive on the meal that we ate last week. We cannot even survive a day without sleep! So how can we survive not embracing everything that we have every single moment?

Embracing difficult relationships is also a part of the parcel because they are enlightening you about your own self and unknowingly forcing you to be stronger and more resilient in your core and maybe that is your personal purpose of life to deal with what life has thrown at you. If you cannot even deal with that, then you are in no way equipped with the skills to deal with more.

Be Yourself

Many wealthy and famous people in the world proclaim that fame and material wealth is not what it takes to be happy. Depression and discomfort still plague celebrities. Always being in the media's eye, judged about everything from strands of their hair to their toenails—it creates an immense pressure on them to always be perfect. They are continually criticized, no matter how much they try or however many expert advisers they hire. There's a heavy demand in their life to please everyone, gain popularity, and find a smashing project to work on. Some celebrities try so hard to be liked that they lose touch with who they are somewhere along the way. They forget what they actually like versus what they are supposed to like, and one little unsupervised move can take attention away from their hard work to them being reduced to a tool for gossip.

The constant need to please people and uphold the fads and trends of a lifestyle are not purely problems of the wealthy and famous. Everyone at some point tries to be someone they are not in order to stroke their own ego.

The ego is the fluff of our existence. As humans, we are conflicted about two realities: one is that life has a purpose; there is God, reincarnation, and we were all created for an unknown reason. On the other hand, the theory of evolution explains how the sun's energy generated the perfect conditions on our planet to produce a single-celled organism, which then evolved into a multi-cell organism that started reproducing, and everything that science has so far been able to theorize. To believe that we all lead a meaningless existence with no consequence, rebirth, or purpose is astonishing. This contradiction is the biggest question in life. Ego is then created to give some meaning to our existence, when in reality, no matter which thesis we arrive at, nothing will make us feel one with ourselves until we are being our utmost authentic self and just focus on being in good spirits always. Whoever helps in soothing our ego becomes our friend and whoever gets in the way of our perceived ideals becomes our enemy.

Due to these contradictory and overwhelming realities that we choose to believe, we develop a mindset that everything has a purpose and if it doesn't, then we must give it one. This is the only life we have, so we must live like it could be gone any minute. We continuously want to be the best in everyone's eyes. We all want to be liked and develop deep-rooted relationships that give meaning to our lives. We seek validation of our existence through others. But that never comes, no matter how hard one tries.

These irrational expectations cause confusion between who others think we should be and who we really are. It leads to disappointment from others when our made-up self is not what they imagine we should be. All the people that we are inspired by or admire in our day-to-day lives are the people who are unique, create their own paths, and are comfortable with what they have to offer. Because they are immersed in pleasing themselves first, they radiate uplifting energy. Their aura is just pleasant to be around, and their validation comes from within.

Being authentic is what makes us unique. It's genuinely the most attractive quality in a person. We should simply be who we are, speak in the language we know, talk the way we want to, and leave people-pleasing attitudes at the door. We should only undertake what we really want to engage in. We should not make false promises or utter things we don't mean. Be true to how you feel for yourself and what you want to do because if you do not address your concerns, no one else will. That is just how life is. Remove the opinions and approval of others from your awareness, so you can realize what you want to create in your intimate life with yourself. When you come to terms with being okay with yourself, then an epiphany frizzles that everyone else in reality is submerged in their own complexities within. No one's opinion or validation has anything on what we feel about ourselves.

Be Happy

In today's world, with an overflow of information, there are infinite sources on how to be happy. Go for a walk, listen to your favourite song, laugh out loud, eat your favourite dish, or simply pick up the phone and speak to an old acquaintance and ask them how they are. Like there are many reasons to be sad, there are equally enough reasons to swing your mood to feel pleasant. Being happy is simply a choice and it takes effort. It isn't being corny if you indulge in being a happy person, despite all the adversities and challenges. It takes courage, self-control, and some serious introspection and that in itself is commendable and rare.

> *"Happiness is a virtue, not its reward."*
> *—Baruch Spinoza*

Chapter Three

Mistakes

"Your trials did not come to punish you,
but to awaken you . . ." —*Paramahansa Yogananda*

Perfection

In their uncertainty about life, people seek advice from an astrologer, tarot reader, or spiritual guru to guide them to the path of light. They hope to take calculated steps to walk the path to success and avoid any mistakes along the way, and if they've made mistakes, they can hide them by performing remedial rituals.

Why are we so glued to the idea of perfection in how we define our lives? Everyone has a different view of perfection. What is perfect to a ten-year-old might be different from what is perfect to a sixty-five-year-old.

What is perfect to a girl might be different from what is perfect to a guy, and what is perfect to a European might be different from what is perfect to an Asian.

Lately, our perfectionism is based on the items we possess and activities we can be seen doing. We want to appear to be living a better life than others, especially those we are unintentionally competing against. Then, other people hold the same standards of themselves and attempt to be even better than us. We are continually trying to one-up them by chasing our irrational idea of perfection and success. This is what we call a *rat race*.

This mindset is not limited to material possessions; it can also penetrate people's lives through the relationships they uphold for everyone to like and comment upon. Our benchmark of perfection comes from the high regard in which we hold others in our life. Jealously, competition, and a conformist mindset result from the value we put on others.

It's common for us to know how to live in the least emotionally draining way possible, yet somehow our actions don't align with our mind's awareness. It's like the wire between the brain, heart, and mouth is missing or has been chopped off. We may understand the wise words that we read or hear, but somehow, we are unable to apply those through our actions or thoughts. These ideas surrounding perfectionism lead us to make mistakes that sabotage us from realizing our full potential.

There are three kinds of mistakes: having a sense of superiority complex, focusing on others, and taking ourselves and our lives too seriously. Harmful actions and hurtful words are acts of naivete. If one is trying to sabotage another's reputation, business, or family, then the outcome is simple: what goes around, comes around. As Isaac Newton's third law of motion states, for every action, there is an equal and opposite reaction. Our own insecurities that we project upon on others will come back to us in the form of the people we attract. We will continually encounter people who make us jealous or insecure because our mind's area of focus is inviting those qualities.

Dealing with Naïve Individuals

Naïve people haven't had the opportunity to grow or learn yet. They are often the quickest to pass judgments upon others and the world. They may classify people with less money or fewer opportunities as less deserving, and they are quick to assume another's identity is attached to their outlook. Some are born with a silver spoon and have spent their lives in a very cushioned environment and these people are the first to live in fear of what others think of them; their world revolves around struggles that might be a dream life for many. They may not realize their naivete, which is why they feel victimized by everything around them.

It's difficult for naïve individuals to find happiness. They always find a reason to undermine their life or self-worth even if they believe they possess everything they could want. It's in their nature to cause a struggle within themselves, like they are stuck in a hamster wheel of desires. They are so oblivious to cause and effect logic that introducing them to a more inclusive way to perceive life is a demanding task. They can be so stubborn that they end up not just hurting internally, but that pain becomes an obligation for others to deal with. They are so troubled inside that it is hard for them to fall asleep or digest food, which affects their ability to live a fuller life.

I believe that if someone has a negative outlook and attitude on the outside, it will definitely cause an issue on the inside as well. If an individual is challenging to exist around, they will have some internal health problems, whether it's digestion or blood pressure. Since it's hard for them to digest life, it becomes hard for them to digest food. They are unaware that they have such energy blockages that they find themselves in similar patterns of life. Even if their situation changes, they are somehow never able to strive for a better self or become content with who they are and what they have. The mind is not even aware of the beautiful life they already have.

The only way to deal with such people is to take a higher road and simply tolerate them. Instead of trying to change them, amp up your self-love barriers to protect your mindset. Holding them accountable is redundant because their victim mentality prevents them from lending any credibility toward others. It's like dealing with two- or three-year-old's; they just haven't become sensible people yet.

They are not evil; they are simply naïve and ignorant. They don't need you to rescue them, and it's not your job to, either. Your job is to observe and choose when to act or not react. Being pained by their actions or words will be of no significance to them. They will always be defensive, vindictive, and lack compassion, as evidenced by the words they utter in every situation.

Dealing with them shouldn't be subjective; it should be very objective. It's easier to deal with naïve people since they don't have two faces; they only have one face of completely being obnoxious. There is no need to get back at them because they are so absorbed in their own thoughts and emotions, and they'll be caught in these patterns forever.

So, why do these individuals cross our path so often? It's because most people are naïve to some extent, and we allow ourselves to be controlled by our emotions. The difference is these people lack this control over themselves. They have no self-discipline, no introspection, and the chords between their brain, soul, and heart aren't connected. Even if they try to think good thoughts or know how to be sensitive and wise, they haven't built a smooth internal path to let it flow and lead them toward a higher frequency of living.

Dealing with Superiority Complexes

When our thoughts don't align with our actions, it's called delusion. Most people struggle in life to be linear inside, and that is okay. It's up to us to realize the effect other people have on us and not let others dump their baggage on us. If we are always getting threatened or affected by people's negativity, in that case, we will end up exhibiting the same mindset, behaviours, and patterns, and we will be another hamster in the hamster wheel joining the hamster club.

Having a sense of superiority complex means that one believes they are special, and their situation is unique compared to others. However, this is a false identity. When we look above, the sky is endless, the stars are countless, and life's possibility is infinite. Thinking that we are superior to other humans because of any attribute like education or finances is like an ant thinking that it has conquered the earth by holding onto a grain of rice. No one is special, no one knows better, and no one is more deserving than others. It is all a mere form of existence, and one is not better without the other. Having a superiority complex is interesting because it is so baseless and untrue. It's just caused by bad parenting to a kid who refuses to grow up.

Sometimes, when we deal with people who have a superiority complex, we make our own little mistakes along the way. We make them a subject and not an object in our lives and by that, I mean we make resolving our conflicts with them our main focus and get off track from our inner path of wisdom. We forget the wise words we have read and forget to step back, analyze, and detach ourselves from someone else's baggage. Certain adversities open us up to different mindsets. They can allow us to better understand another's situation, which makes us empathetic and sympathetic toward them. As we grow, so do our sensitivities. However, people trapped within their own mental frames and who resist the growth from their experiences limit themselves, which is what they tend to attract—similar people and experiences into their orbit. That's how economists base their predictions too. A potential rate of return is dependent on the investment's utility. So, when we are dealing with insensitive people who have a superiority complex, then we are engaging in futile behaviour that isn't self-serving.

Living in constant competition with others or having a snobbish mentality only limits us from unlocking our full potential of love. It's the mistake that we have all made at some point in our lives. Having a superiority complex isn't helping us become superior in any form. Rather, it limits us from even being understood.

Many of my friends with wealthy parents or who have had sudden monetary success have a superiority complex. They consider themselves better than others because of their purchasing power, but in reality, they did not earn that power, so it's a fragile complex. Some people have a superiority complex because of their physical attributes, but once they open their mouths, it gets difficult to even have a human let alone intellectual conversations with them. Others think they are superior because of their jobs or the money they make, yet they are so toiled up in that complex that they are some of the most uncharitable and miserly humans on earth. They get so protective about their wealth that they think everyone wants them for their money, which prevents them from building a real emotional bond with people.

What we think makes us superior starts working against us, one way or the other. No one is superior. Everyone has the same beating heart, and everyone is breathing from the same air. If you feel validated by the stuff you own, then it's not your doing. It's the artists and the engineers who built that stuff, and it doesn't make anyone else superior. However, it should enlighten us to how wonderful our world is and how our existence is irrelevant without everyone in this life together. Everything in our world is truly a team effort.

If we live with this delusion of superiority, we further ourselves away from who we could be. We don't end up living our life. At some point, we all end up living in delusions and made-up hypothetical nonsense that isn't benefitting us at all. But we can't give in because it leads to an emptiness that continually needs to be filled. This could cause us to engage more in behaviours that showcase that superiority, and that brings me to our second mistake: focusing our energies on others.

Too Much Focus on Others

Today's world is designed in a way that we are unknowingly giving our energy away to the people we know and even to the ones we don't know anything about. We are social media stalkers who want to know what celebrities wore at which event or who is having an affair with whom. We are unintentionally curious about others, which causes us to have random dreams about random people. Have you ever noticed that the horrific crap we watch on television sometimes pops up randomly in our dreams?

We overlook the basic fact that we are all energies in the form of perishable bones and flesh. The energy that flows in our body decides our health and the energy that flows in our mind creates our life. When we read a good thought of the day, it has a magical power to uplift our mindset, which further dictates our actions throughout the day. Falling in love is so powerful that everything seems glorious and worth living for.

As much as we forget how mindful we need to be of our unique energy, we unknowingly scatter that energy every single second. We disperse our powers every day. Human beings have an immense brain capacity to store information, like the thoughts we create that dictate our behaviours. Even though the capacity is immense, it's not infinite. When we choose to surrender our energy to other people, we are not living our life. We are living theirs.

When I was little, my paternal aunt told me a story of a king who was busy and frustrated at the time and had shunned a saint away who approached him looking for food. The saint quietly left, and after a few days, when the king was out in the forest to hunt an exotic animal, he noticed a very brightly lit tent in the middle of nowhere. The king's curiosity took him inside that tent, and he found the saint he had treated poorly, floating mid-air in a meditative state.

Upon witnessing the divinity, the king realized that the man he had dismissed was truly someone special, and he needed to make it up to him. He expressed his remorse to the saint and requested redemption. The saint told the king that forgiveness alone wouldn't undo his sin, but the king himself needed to correct his actions. The saint pointed at the heap of horse's turds and said, "Eat this pile to erase your sins. What you sow, so shall you reap. Your behaviour was the opposite of kindness, so you must eat the opposite of food to clear your karma."

The king couldn't eat the horse's feces and asked for an alternate way to undo the sin he had committed. The saint gave him the best advice he could. He said, "Make your kingdom's citizens criticize you. Make everyone say negative things about you, and this heap will start disappearing."

The king agreed, then paraded around the city on his elephant with a prostitute while drinking heavily. He'd smash bottles and verbally abuse the people walking on the streets. Shortly enough, people started to despise the king and would criticize him behind his back. Slowly, the heap of horse's turds started disappearing. The king went back to the saint to ask how everyone's ire against him had erased the pile? The saint explained that every time someone spoke negatively of him, they took the king's sins upon themselves. The moral of the story was that negative discussion about others brings out their negativity in our behaviour, and eventually in our lives.

> *"Whoever fights monsters should see to it that in*
> *the process he does not become a monster."*
> *—Friedrich Nietzsche*

Judging others and indulging in gossip only fills our minds with our perceptions of those people. This brings their vibrations and karma into our lives. It's a wicked pattern to free ourselves from because we tend to judge the one who is judging them. We judge each other and condemn each other's deeds at an unrelenting rate. We habitually come to hasty conclusions without doing much research and speculation of our own.

A mango's taste can be described as sweet with a juicy texture and tightly packed pulp that melts in the mouth. However, until we bite a mango, we won't be able to feel or understand its taste. Experience is the best way to obtain knowledge. We must experience an event, situation, personality, food, or anything else in life to understand its physical, emotional, and in some cases, spiritual aspects.

We can never fully understand others, and we shouldn't waste time trying. It's easier to accept others for who they are and be appreciative of it. Everyone outside of us is our teacher, and we should respect the ones who challenge us and bring out the best in us. If someone is bringing out the worst in us, it's not them; it's us because that is all we have inside ourselves. How we train ourselves to act toward people and situations is entirely our responsibility. Blaming others for being a certain way is like blaming the salt for being too salty and sugar for being too sweet. It's irrelevant, and we are only ruining our minds and wasting energy that we should be using to better ourselves. No matter how much of one's enlightening wisdom is shared, others won't understand its significance until they experience it. A teacher can teach a pupil about a subject, but it's the student who has to write the exam. If they don't pick up the textbook and get some practice, they are bound to fail.

When we pass judgment on others, we are speculating based on our own experiences, a conclusion about someone else's behaviour, characteristics, future, past, present, family, background, goals, and capabilities. We use our mental capacity to form our biased judgments and then share them with others. With its negative, condescending, and judgmental connotation, this gossip is not only harming us on an energetic level, but also helping that person clean their turds!

As we grow older, the ability to be in the moment mentally and spiritually reduces because the mind, over time, collects so much baggage. After working long hours, running errands, and catering to our social obligations, we sometimes waste the small amount of our remaining energy stalking others on social media or gossiping. We should instead use this energy to better ourselves and our interactions with anyone outside of us.

The biggest sin one can commit is to think negatively about others. When an artist paints a sunset on the canvas, it will never replicate the exact sunset. Instead, it shows the craft of the artist. What we say about others does not portray who those people are. Instead, it reveals how we perceive others and what type of filter we use.

If you can't say it to their face, don't speak it behind their back. This constant need to make oneself feel better is a rationale of a fool because they are not focusing their mind on themselves. Instead, they allow other people's lives to occupy their energy. Whether it is good or bad, don't let other people take up your energy. It takes many lifetimes to restore our energy to a point where we are free from emotions, happenings, relationships, greed, and temporary wants of temporary human life. We are fools to waste our precious and limited energy on this planet on others.

Honestly, we all have the personality of this naïve fool within us. We all have been naïve and foolish in different stages of our lives and maybe still are in day-to-day experiences. We easily forget our learned wisdom and get caught by our loose hold on our minds. We come across such people in our lives because that is who we are at the moment. We are the ones who invited those thoughts and behaviours that we feel from others.

Taking Ourselves Too Seriously

"If you think you're enlightened, go and spend a week with your family." —Ram Dass

The truth is, conflict is a part of life, and we have conflicts with everyone, from our parents to our school friends to people in our periphery. We will always have disagreements and differences in opinions, but that does not define our lives or our character. How we act toward them does, and it could be as simple as having respect for their existence. If those people didn't exist, then our perspective would not be this evolved. They gave us something to introspect upon, and with that, an opportunity to grow. This brings me to our third mistake: taking ourselves and our lives too seriously.

Most machines need an oil change to run smoothly. We are the most intelligent machine on this planet, and even we need a constant change in our thoughts. Steel is more commonly destroyed by its own rust than anything else. Similarly, we are not destroyed by anyone else other than our own mindset and beliefs.

Like everything else in life, beliefs must also be changed and updated to match our experiences. This isn't to say that what others do doesn't affect us—it does, and it is supposed to. But it is not limited to the obvious effect that causes self-victimization. We take ourselves, our jobs, the people around us, and our materialistic possessions too seriously. It's as if there is nothing beyond it.

What we believed yesterday might not be applicable today, and what we learn today might not be applicable tomorrow. When we endure emotional pain, we get so attached to that pain that we find comfort in being hurt. Letting go of it seems like an impossible task, but slowly, with time, things change. The dust settles, and what seems too terrible right now might be a blessing for the future. Being adaptable and flexible in life makes us limitless. We limit ourselves by adopting a fixed set of beliefs and responses to life and always behaving and reacting from the same old patterns. Do not confuse your imposed limitations on you as a part of your identity; it is not. Your identity lies in your abilities.

Nothing Lasts Forever

"Awakening is not changing who you are but discarding who you are not." —Deepak Chopra

My dad's brother was a very vicious man. He wanted to rob my dad of our ancestral property and wanted us, my dad's kids, to not succeed in life. He spent his entire life holding grudges and ignoring that he was the biggest jerk due to his mindset's fury. He was very attached to the property, jewellery, money, and his own branch of the family that he felt that everyone else isn't worthy of humanitarian treatment. When he was younger, he used to snatch things from his siblings so he could possess them. He was such an injured soul that he thought everyone owed him due to his superiority complex.

In reality, he was covering up his deep-rooted insecurities. One of his sons had a serious mental condition while the other had physical issues, and he was jealous that his nephews and nieces didn't have these same difficulties. He aggressively kept trying to prove he was superior to others, and one day his organs just stopped working and he also lost his vision. The property he was fighting so hard for turned on him, and all the money he had saved up for a rainy day could not save his life.

That is it; that is life. It's here one day, and it is gone tomorrow. The same applies to our relationships with others. There is no need to hold such futile grudges against each other since no one exists forever. We are all the same flesh and bones. We all have to coexist, not co-depend. Codependency is when you need other people to exist, and those other people are in control of how you feel. In that situation, we unknowingly give our power away.

If you do not like something about another person, talk to them like you would want to be spoken to. Don't justify your anger because it's going to come back to you. Self-love is when you hold yourself to the highest regard and standard as well.

We shouldn't hold grudges against people who have hurt us or if we believe things have not gone our way. We hold on to those occurrences so fearfully that the fear and stress destroy us. When we give our power away to things, people, materials, and money, they will always enslave us. We won't be enjoying those delights. Instead, we will be working to keep them in our lives, and we will always be struggling. Challenges are a part of life, and if we let every little thing dictate our mood, then we will never grow, and we will surely never be happy or free. We will always be a prisoner in the cage of our own limitations.

Coexisting peacefully seems like an art of the past. We have forgotten how to be accepting of others while at the same time keeping a sense of detachment. The North Star in the sky was a map for humans back in the day to follow their path to a free world. A free world that entailed no slavery and where there was an opportunity to be free from society and its pressures. We all want the freedom just to exist and make sense of our little life through doing and learning.

Don't depend on people seeking forgiveness or wait on them to right their wrongs. Accept it and thank them for opening an element inside of you that you had been guarding. Say thank you to all your bullies, all your haters, and all the people who made you think you were any less than them. Wish them luck and leave

Divneet Kaur

them with your best wishes to overcome their need to feed their ego at the expense of others.

Nobody has it all figured out, and no one else knows how to live your life better than you do. No one else is in control of your mind but you. If we are aware of these mistakes that we make daily, it's easier for us to catch ourselves and modify our mindset and behaviour. It's not easy, and it takes practice for a good attitude to become a habit that is not forced. We are not perfect, and we all make mistakes. To sit and dwell in our imperfection has no significance. Instead, actively initiating a fruitful thought followed by a productive action will help us get past our regrets.

If you want others to forgive you for your mistakes, forgive others first. If you want others to love the imperfect you, love the imperfections of others first. Life is too short to take it too seriously and make a big deal out of every little thing. The bigger picture should always be to live and act the best you can. No, it's not okay to convince yourself that it is okay to be upset and depressed all the time. The very reason you are depressed is because of you, and the very barrier between you and happiness is yourself. Life is too short to make a big deal out of your happiness or your sadness. Science plays a few tricks on us too where there is at times a chemical imbalance due to an underlying health or mental condition that inhibits us from living our best, every possible second; however, in today's world, the resources are plenty for everyone to get guidance or assistance in the event they are medically suffering and those resources must be utilized, not just for self, but also for the sake of others. At the end of the day, it boils down to taking responsibility for ourselves and recognizing that it is only us that eventually holds the key to the door within.

We actively make mistakes when we think we are better than others and deserve a more righteous treatment. In truth, we are not in control of how others act toward us, but we can control how we act toward others. We give away our precious and limited energy to others rather than using it for our own good. Every day, we miss opportunities to see the best in everyone so that we can fill our mind's cup with the good.

Life shouldn't be taken so seriously that we only live through our limited ego. Life is not permanent, and neither are our beliefs nor our opinions. My dad always says, "Do good, have good." The mistake of allowing others to occupy our minds and remaining in competition with the haves and have-nots only undermines ourselves. The sooner we open our minds to the power of our sensitivity, the quicker we can spend our mind's energy on ourselves so we can use it to its fullest potential.

Let go of noises about others in your head and let go of seeking negativity in others. It serves no purpose other than self-harm. Our mind is precious, and we must take care of it by surrounding ourselves with people who uplift us while also being the person who uplifts others. Break free from these basic mistakes to truly live your life and carve out the uniqueness within you.

Chapter Four

Narcissism

*"By three methods we may learn wisdom: First,
by reflection, which is noblest; Second, by imitation,
which is easiest; and third by experience,
which is the bitterest." —Confucius*

When we humans use our physical bodies to commit a wrongful and hateful deed, it is called a crime and is subjected to legal consequences because it can be seen and felt by others, but when we brew malefic, hateful, and condescending thoughts in our minds, those unseen thoughts become our sins; no one else can witness them and they are truly ours to behold. They present themselves as challenges to our own happiness and serenity. The unmentored and uncensored thoughts create a narcissist demon within us who is reluctant to free itself from itself. There is a reason our history is full of slavery because there is a certain beauty in being controlled by the authority. It allowed us to hold the other person responsible for our fate and control our behaviours. People worshipped such personalities who could mobilize the crowd by instilling fear, imposing their vision and purpose on others. Even though the world is continually evolving politically, on personal levels, we enslave ourselves voluntarily to the commanding dictator within and of others. There is a narcissist in all of us. We dilute our behaviour and communication with how we feel, and we tend to take ourselves too seriously, undermining everyone else's feelings. The number of grudges we hold toward others is the exact amount of narcissism within us. We want to be forgiven and understood but have not exhibited that within our own behaviours. Forgiving others for their selfish or unsought after actions, even without them asking for forgiveness, can save us a lot of mind space that we could use to serve our greater self instead of a little fearful crippled narcissist within us.

We embrace emotional abuse so much that somewhere, unknowingly, we implement it into our own characters. Think of all the things you do not like others doing to you, for example: if someone in their body language or words belittles you regarding your financial status and shows off their wealth or their spending power, then in turn, you compete with that person to be even wealthier and that very competitive urge to earn the same wealth in the process makes you too become snobbish of your possessions because those were earned to verify your identity. Our narcissism comes from our own personal conflicts, and it is important to take note of whenever others ignite the inferiority within us.

A narcissist is a slave to someone else and that someone else is a slave to another. The chain and cycle are never-ending until we decipher the expectations we impose on others and on our destinies to relieve us of an unexplained pain. The truth is, it is not anyone else or our destinies. It is us and our present moment that has the key to unlock the chains of our internal freedom. Inner freedom is when we are not dependent on others or materialistic possessions to validate us, but we ourselves are secure enough to live and create our best selves.

Our opinions, way of life, understanding of the almighty, and worldly desires are all subjective and a result of our experiences. Our unique needs and wants are a result of what serves us and what we emphasize. To live a good life, all we need is a healthy mind, food on the table, medicine for ailments, four walls to keep us safe, and a means to keep ourselves occupied. Anything more than that is just our greed. We can still have higher ambitions, but if we define our happiness by chasing tangible things, we can never be humble. We will always brag to make us feel like we have achieved something because that is how we have validated others.

A narcissist is a person who has a superiority complex and considers themselves special. They expect to have their way with everyone around them, and if it doesn't go the way they expect, it's an opportunity to criticize. Their fertile inhibitions take over their reality. We all want the right things said and done to us. We all want the right outcomes, relationships, and careers. Most importantly, we want to have a significant status in others' perceptions of us.

We must first understand that no matter how big our struggles or challenges are, everyone is fighting their personal battles. It's a part of life. We cannot overlook that fact and punish others with our inner upheaval. When things don't go our way, we get frustrated and immediately blame other people for our frustration. We will always find people who talk rather than listen, who judge what others are doing, and who need to have the last word. If they cannot have the last word, they will make stuff up based on their own paradigms to justify the mindless attitudes and then they blame others for distancing themselves or becoming complacent. In my Indian culture, narcissism is a bit much and my few Indian people love to believe that they are the gifts on this planet and that they are better and more deserving than everyone else. That attitude always makes them suffer to which they remain oblivious. This chapter is specifically dedicated to them, and everyone like them.

Respect Differences

Letting others' behaviour dictate how we should feel is narcissistic because we expect that they should only behave in a way that pleases us. Fishes live in water, alligators can live on both land and water, and birds fly in the air. Different wild animals have different needs and capabilities, and different trees exist in different climates. Different fields of work address different concerns and opinions. Our world is our world because of the differences we behold and the faculties we adhere to.

I have seen many silly quarrels amongst people. A young driver in a rush might cuss at the driver in front of them for driving slowly. They may not realize that the other driver has a headache or could be a cautious older driver. Diversity is the core of our nature. Different elements in nature compound together to produce different results. Everyone is born different, thinks differently, and has different priorities. No two human beings have matching fingerprints, even if they are twins. We are made up of differences. Our schools are comprised of education that masters different fields. Having differences with people is powerful. It is needed to produce visions, goals, and ideals for one another.

Would we love our lives if everyone in the world was an exact replica of us? It would surely not be interesting. The idea that the world belongs to us isn't true, but we do belong to the world. We have forgotten to be humble. We are not alive because of our efforts, but because of the air we breathe, the genes that we inherited, and the family, religion, and culture we were born into. However, when something good comes along, we brag about it or hold it too dearly.

We feel that everyone should do things as per our liking and convenience. We feel betrayed when our friends or family members do not abide by our idea of reciprocation. We get emotionally hurt and carry that baggage with us, which sometimes causes us to act passive-aggressively.

We all have to live our lives and deal with our specific challenges. Everyone's life is different, and so are everyone's mindsets. What we may make big in our head might not even be noticed by someone else. They might not be aware that their actions are hampering our feelings. All of us think from the standpoint of blamers. We blame how someone's actions made us feel, how we have been shaped, and how our past experiences have affected our behaviour today.

The truth is, other people's behaviours are just a reflection of who we are on the inside. If we are insecure, we will always try harder to be approved by others by showing them the stuff we own or our experiences. Our insecure behaviour can either come across as sycophancy or exhibit the opposite of humility. We boast about what is special in our life by showing off, and then when the other person does not consider us because of our very attitude of self-conceitedness, our feelings get hurt.

We were given life before we developed cognitive abilities. Our limbs, senses, hair, and body were already gifts when we were born. We should use them to expand our existence rather than diverting the focus on accumulating pride and defining ourselves. No one is special. Everyone is a human with the same heart and brain. The path each one of us chooses to walk is different. If we define our expectations in terms of material items instead of doing something that uplifts others, or if we desire to be liked by others instead of liking ourselves, we are bound to create outward, desperate emotions that only make us mediocre.

Listen

Some people believe it's okay to "say it like it is" or utter the first thing that comes to their mind to fulfill that itch of being heard. It's a very insensitive thing to do because we wouldn't appreciate if it was done to us. Conflict resolution shouldn't be an ego battle. It should be about communicating a message instead of expecting other people to automatically understand what we are thinking or feeling.

If we are always talking and not listening, it surely makes it harder for us to hear the other person and understand where they are coming from. Maybe we can help them better by grasping what they care about. We should still express ourselves and share our thoughts, but sometimes understanding a person isn't just about a conversation. It's also about being patient and letting time show us what they do instead of what they say.

If we all were all patient with each other and let our personalities develop apart from the expectations imposed on us, it'd help us all coexist and enjoy each other's company. If we want people to be patient with us through our difficult times, which might be taxing on them, it is equally our responsibility to be patient and give people time to come into their own.

There may be facets of others that we do not like; for example, an authoritative boss or an aggressive partner. We must first make sure not to embrace their harsh ways and understand that they are dealing with something within themselves. They are likely not aware of the impact of their attitude on others. In those situations, it's better to be silent than make it more complicated since they will only understand what they want to understand.

When verbal communication becomes frustrating, it's an opportunity to remove yourself from the situation, recognize that the other person is challenging, then step back. Let them say what they utter, and if no one aligns with their ways and wants, maybe just slightly, they will want to listen.

There will be times when people will not understand you, and you will not understand everyone either. Therefore, we shouldn't jump to a conclusion and start despising them. It's an opportunity to take another route and just be present. Be aware that their behaviour has nothing to do with you; it's how they are wired. Remain detached, and don't develop negative feelings. The right opportunity will present itself, and it comes from practising everyday mindfulness of where to speak and knowing where you won't be heard.

Don't Give In to Anxiety

All family comedic drama soaps are about people facing everyday problems and still enjoying life with chirpy music in the background. In a murder mystery, the background music is so intense that it brings the audience to the edge of their seats. You are the writer, director, and background score of your story. It's up to you to select the music you want to play in the background. You get to decide what you want to draw from every experience. Accepting a part of you that is not serving any good in your life will not do you any good in the end if you let it continue.

For instance, being anxious about situations in life and accepting your anxious responses is only going to make it harder for you to deal with a situation. Every situation will only give you more anxiety because once we create that in our minds, we create it in our actions. It's bound to exist in our reality because the element of anxiety has control of every situation. Even favourable results are not going to resolve our anxiety.

Everything we do eventually becomes a habit and part of us. Life is about challenges; if we always react to them with stress and made-up pride nonsense, we will piss off the people around us by being so difficult to deal with. Then, we will end up with impractical results that will make us labour further to correct them or keep them afloat.

We Are Dependent on Each Other

We believe we are thinking for ourselves, but we are truly not thinking of ourselves or others. We survive because others sacrifice for us, firstly our mothers who go through so much pain, then both parents who do their best to put food on our table. We have friends who make us laugh, teachers who educate us, grocery store employees and farmers to keep us fed, and all sorts of other people who are working hard worldwide to produce our clothing and other services.

Everyone is working for each other, and everything is dependent on each other. We cannot let our emotions take over so much that we believe we're suffering through something unique, and everyone should feel the impact of our moods. No one owes us anything. We are indebted to all of the people around us who play a role in who we are. A sense of compassion and respect should be our default way of interacting with people.

If you let a part of your personality control you, it not only impacts your life but also impacts others. It's narcissism because if we do not appreciate the value of others' lives, how would we appreciate our own? We don't deserve to be cared for either.

Don't Be a Know-It-All

We limit ourselves so much by being a know-it-all. We get fixated on our behavioural patterns and our mindsets, not realizing the vastness of this universe. The sun is hot, whereas Pluto is dead cold. Learning about others and understanding differences brings us closer to wholeness. Being flexible and having a dynamic mindset makes us like water that can take any form and shape, which is why the majority of our earth is filled with it. It's in our hands how others treat us. If we only talk instead of listening, impose expectations, and flaunt our know-it-all attitude, then we are bound to dilute all our relationships. More importantly, we are draining ourselves of the love and respect that we could create and receive.

I used to work at an entry-level position in a software-based business. Whenever a product didn't flow from point A to point B and vice versa in perfect order, it would make me believe that my superiors or people in different departments weren't doing their job properly. I believed they were incompetent until I moved through the different departments and realized how the grass isn't greener on the other side. There is always more to learn, and there are different levels of priorities within an organization that might not be a priority for other teams.

Every department taught me something new and made me realize that there is deeper knowledge behind everything. If something seems complicated, it might be due to inabilities within the software's coding logic. Learning about the various pieces of that puzzle made me a better tech-support agent to solve others' (and my own) problems. This ultimately made me a better employee.

A know-it-all attitude isn't very progressive or cool, yet somehow influential individuals have made it seem cool. They wanted to be superior or to create a market for themselves and be desirable members of society. It doesn't work that way. It's a lot to indulge in, and quite frankly, is unfulfilling and limiting.

Instead, we must take that power and feel proud of ourselves for wanting to know it all and put ourselves in situations that educate us more. Being open-minded, learning or trying new ways, being patient, and listening to how others perceive us will only present opportunities for us to learn more about life.

If everything must go exactly the way we desire, we are limiting ourselves from new ways of enjoying life. Instead, we repeat the same old patterns and expect miraculous results overnight. We want to feel safe, calm, and understood. It's not someone else's responsibility to make us feel that way; it is ours. We can't be so self-consumed and navigate life as a "my way or the highway" kind of an attitude. Sometimes, others might know a shortcut or a fun way to get to a destination.

Consider *What Really Matters*

When I look back at my childhood and adolescence, I wish I was more fun and made more friends instead of quarrelling over silly things that did not matter. I wish I hadn't tried to appear exclusive by exhibiting arrogance and hadn't outsmarted some really cool people. I could have had so much more fun if I wasn't so uptight.

And as we grow old, we all look back and wonder if we could have had more fun, or lived our childhood a bit longer, or loved a little harder. All the other stuff that mattered back then is of no relevance today. Only how we behaved, reacted, loved, and supported each other matters. If our background music is the tune of love and good energy, then we will shed our uptight ideas and learn to uplift ourselves and others around us at all times.

We must realize how important, impactful, and everlasting the memories of how we felt in a situation are rather than what material objects we owned. Only then can we open our spirit to the power and reverence of thoughts that go through our mind and body.

Nobody owes us anything, and we are by no means better than others. Always tooting our own horns is only inviting increased insecurities and more delusions that we have accustomed ourselves to. The power that the intangible holds is incomparable to the tangible. The fact we place so much importance on it is narcissistic, vain, and serves no purpose. Simplicity and wanting to know more are truly the coolest things a human can possess. It makes us look back and feel proud that we lived a little.

Chapter Five

Food for Thought . . .

*"A healthy man wants a thousand things,
a sick man only wants one." —Confucius*

DIEting

There's an overload of advice regarding optimal dietary needs today, ranging from keto diets to intermittent fasting or simply how we should start our day. Some experts suggest we need three to five litres of water per day, but (not-so) fun fact, did you know some people are actually allergic to water? Some say we require specific amounts of protein and carbs. Others recommend having more green leafy vegetables with red meat, while in contrast, some advocate for no meat at all! Choosing a proper health regimen can be overwhelming.

This overload of choices has caused our personal diet to become a controversial topic. We may eat a certain way at home, but when we eat at a restaurant with other people, we try to make healthier choices. We emphasize our wants more than our needs, which is why we have health problems and even massive and avoidable monetary debts.

For example, chia seeds are high in fibre, and consuming them with lemon water can supposedly help reduce weight. But what if they're not available locally? How much would you be willing to pay to get them? In North American and European grocery stores, we can find all kinds of vegetables and fruits from around the globe all year round, seasonal and non-seasonal. We often buy foreign items, sometimes with a high price tag, because we see an online post advertising its benefits. This blessing to have one-stop grocery stores is something we take for granted. This expansive selection of food choices will spoil our future generations, who likely won't consider where and how the food is grown, who it is grown by, and what it really does to our bodies. Having grocery stores with all the produce is another thing most of us take for granted; meanwhile, it is not even a phenomenon in some parts of the globe.

With the age of information pollution from eating this to that, we overcomplicate our machine by feeding it complex protein powders or other apparently health-boosting substitutes that come in jars or bottles. The answer to every little ache or twitch is searched on the internet, which invariably suggests cancer or tumours and that over-heightened fear of being sick that we try to run away from, becomes a blockage in our mental health. The fear has no place if we indulge ourselves in everyday healthy and simple practices and not partake in them with the fear of falling sick. Some supremely health-oriented folks who have worried all their lives about their health have passed away before time; meanwhile, people who have emphasized very little to themselves the importance of health and have lived with a certain level of ignorance, and a positive attitude toward food, are still alive in their nineties.

Our existence, by default, is terminal. Falling sick or developing faulty tissues in our body over time is a part of aging and being a human. It happens to most of us, sometimes mild and other times severe. Fear and denoting negativity toward ailments aren't going to help them heal but moving forward with self-care, acceptance, and positive actions can heal broken emotions, which in turn help the body to cope with distress. Fasting is one of the most beautiful and simplest methods of discarding our inner weaknesses. Don't be such a slave to your hunger. When our body doesn't get food, it eats its own cells and the first ones to go are the weakest ones and it is paradoxical because the same applies to human beings. Do not give your negative aspects more fuel than you already do. If it doesn't get energized, it will find a way to discard itself. Don't be so obsessed by food that it is consumed out of desperation; consume it to energize you. Not that it is the answer to all illnesses, but when we forgo a meal once in a while, maybe someone else will get fed our share.

"Nothing is more fatal to health than an over care of it." —Benjamin Franklin

Non-Vegetarianism

I used to be a non-vegetarian and loved my mom's exquisite black pepper chicken to the core. It was my go-to meal every time I needed comfort or a lavish dinner. However, once I started questioning the meat's origin, purpose, and effect on my body, it didn't tempt me as much as it once did.

Centuries ago, when there were no grocery stores as we know them now, the availability of food depended on the environment and season. Malls and colossal skyscrapers didn't occupy the earth. There used to be vast stretches of rural land that people would pilgrimage through or fight battles on. At the time, the only way to eat was to hunt an animal, skin it, and then consume it right away. Meat stays in the digestive system longer due to its complex compounds so that one would feel satisfied for longer in dire situations of survival.

Meat choices varied based on the territory, like bison in cold regions or fish in tropical regions. These animals were wild and free before they were hunted in their natural environment. They were mentally and physically healthier, so they'd provide more nutritional benefits to those who consumed them. Imagine a free person versus a person in prison; a free individual thrives in their natural element, while a person behind bars is more likely to be depressed and have a stressed body. Similarly, there is a difference in the mental and physical health of animals in their natural and free environment versus animals in cages.

As life evolved and people could go to butchers to buy meat, it was uncommon for people to eat meat every day. Diets consisted of mainly grains and vegetables; meat was only cooked on special occasions. Slowly, with the rise of the free market, meat was sold as if it were a necessity, which up to that point it hadn't been. Businessmen opened factories to mass-produce artificially inseminated animals to fulfill this demand. Animals started taking their first and last breaths in a cage-like environment.

Animals are highly intuitive and survive in the wild by sensing danger and fleeing from situations. When they are raised in a cage, they continuously release a stress hormone known as the adrenocorticotropic hormone, or ACTH. This flows through their entire body and then gets nicely wrapped as chopped meat that we end up consuming. Remember the famous line "we are what we eat"? That might explain why, as a population, humans are increasingly stressed and depressed. Now that meat is commonly eaten for each meal, every day, and the source of the meat isn't natural, we are losing our naturalness in the process.

Focusing on our wants more than our needs is what gets us into trouble. I do not believe that we should completely ban meat or that it's immoral to consume it. However, if you desire meat, research a humane and natural source where you can purchase it and consider not eating meat at every meal. Since meat takes a long time for our digestive system to process, one should avoid stress-induced hormones that can lead to ailments in the core of the body, our gut.

In extremely cold or desert-like regions, where there is limited availability of fresh vegetables, fruits, and grains, diets in those regions may contain more meat out of necessity. However, if meat is being consumed just for the sake of taste and habit, remember it can be deteriorating for your body and mind in the long term because it reflects a lack of awareness and self-control, but no judgment here. We all are learning to unburden ourselves in this maze of life.

Drink Your Water

Another common myth is that drinking many cups of water or herbal tea in a day is ultra-beneficial. Our liver is the organ that processes all of those liquids, and if we are constantly consuming water, green tea, or alcohol, we may be causing it to work too hard. An overworked liver can lead to a higher risk of it malfunctioning or weakening over time.

This is not to say that we should not drink beneficial liquids for our body, just that we should give our body time to rest in between. I believe we should drink an amount of water that's in proportion with our food intake. So, if our bodies are approximately seventy percent water, then we must make it a habit to consume seventy percent water and thirty percent food every day.

Back in the day, water was full of minerals because it came straight from lakes and rivers. We cannot compare the quality to our tap water today. However, I must emphasize that we remain unappreciative of how we can let it run; many parts of the world don't even have this option. Some people still have to go to wells with their buckets and find ways to store that water for days. Many live with the fear of unsanitary water mixing with their freshwater that would risk their health, sometimes resulting in death.

One should be mindful that the human body is predominantly made up of water, and it is essential for its functioning. Not only does water support optimum health and skin, but it is also a natural mood regulator. Water is a natural healer and something that nature has provided us for free as an elixir. No wonder we take it for granted.

Start Your Morning Right

Like we train our minds, we can train our body to ask for water when it's thirsty. We do so by creating positive routines when we drink water. I am a firm believer in starting the day with hot water, and if one wants to jazz it up, adding a freshly squeezed lemon can help cleanse our body thoroughly. In the time we spend waking up while sipping our hot water, we have an opportunity to ignore our cellphones and everything else that chains us. We can simply feed our mind positive affirmations, like how wonderful it is to be breathing and alive for another day. Or consider that today is the day when you are the oldest you have ever been and the youngest you will ever be! That activity not only hypnotizes the molecules of the water with our spell, but also affects our body positively.

When we wake up after a night's sleep, several things are produced in the body that require excretion first thing in the morning. Our internal temperature is organically warm, so warm water aids the digestive tract to cleanse itself effectively. The nutritional properties of the lemon's vitamin C help clean the intestine's walls thoroughly, removing any bacteria or mucus that may have been produced, and nature provides many other herbal ingredients, like lemons, that help in regulating our health, like fennel and cumin seeds, oregano oil, et cetera. Nature has everything for everyone! If this is done religiously, you may find no need to rely on antibiotics to remove bacteria from the stomach.

Water is such a divine blessing that we must start and end our day with it. Drinking water can become an excellent time and an excuse to feed our minds positive beliefs and affirmations.

Relationship Within

When humans act against nature, we cause things like climate change that negatively affects the entire planet. Similarly, you should avoid eating unnatural foods, so you don't sabotage your body. Eating what is easily and affordably available in each season will make it less likely for your food to be infused with preservative chemicals that affect the digestive system. If your digestive system isn't strong, it can really mess up your entire bodily structure. The only way the digestive structure can be strengthened is by eating simple, light, freshly made food. Eating raw fruits for breakfast and throwing some lentils in with brown rice for lunch can really reduce stress on the internal system.

Our body also requires physical movement throughout the day. We are not meant to stare at screens for fifteen hours straight. It not only kills our brain cells but leaves very little room for mindfulness. How does a romantic relationship between a couple grow? By spending time communicating with each other about their feelings. We tend to neglect the one stable relationship in our lives that we have between our body and our mind. Like a relationship with another human, our body and mind need our time to be heard, to be felt, and most importantly, they need adequate rest.

Our relationship with ourselves governs how happy we can keep our two halves—our body and our mind. If our body and mind are healthy and aligned, then we are unstoppable. One of the founders of psychology, Sigmund Freud, theorized that humans have three primary parts of personality, the *id*, the *ego,* and the *superego.* The id fuels our desire for instant gratification with no consideration of the consequences. For example, when a child cries for sugary food and will do anything to get it, they are being motivated by their id. A child doesn't realize that too much sugar is bad for the body and hasn't yet learned the cognitive ability to self-control; the desire is aggressive. As (some) adults develop ego, we know the effects of sugar and can control our intake thanks to our ego. We understand the consequences, so our mind encourages us to make healthy choices by believing in moderation. Superego is a part of us that holds us to the highest standards, morals, and ethics and is extremely judgmental toward who we are.

While we always have that internal voice guiding and leading us, sometimes we all choose to become infants and not care about consequences at all! Eating right before bed means the digestive tract is functioning all night, resulting in the body not getting appropriate rest. The next day, when your alarm clock buzzes at 6:00 a.m., it's your id that motivates you to hit that snooze button until 9:00 a.m. That decision may cause you not to accomplish any goals that day, which turns into negative self-belief thoughts that eventually give in to a bottle of wine that night to rinse and repeat the next day.

This isn't to say we should make food before bed a faux pas. Sometimes it happens but balancing other details effortlessly in the day can be ingeniously self-preserving. Luckily, it takes minimal effort for us to witness some magical changes, and it all starts with tweaking little habits day after day.

Our body requires food to function, and it needs food that fuels it instead of exhausting it. Feeding the body complex cereals with milk for breakfast can be very tasty and convenient, but we should take better care of our bodies. It can be an easier task when we understand that every time we eat food, it is to fuel our body and not just to satisfy our greedy taste buds.

Eat light, eat when your body is hungry, eat lentils, grains, vegetables, fruits, and nuts, and don't harass yourself with calorie counting. Natural substances don't have drastic side effects, so eat them guilt-free and create a positive association with food intake. Many people resist nutrient-rich food and turn to vitamin-rich medicines instead. It's a perfect example of how misunderstood nature is and how big of control freaks we can be!

Body and Mind

Keep in mind what works for one person might not work for someone else because everyone has their own needs and organic desires. The body loves certain intakes and will reflexively ask for them. Do not mindlessly follow everything that you read on the internet; observe what your body needs. At times, our bodies may not align with our minds because we treat our minds and bodies differently.

In Ayurveda, a holistic practice of wellness, there is the belief if something is wrong with the mind, that indicates something is wrong with the body. Likewise, if something is wrong with the body, then something is wrong with the mind. In this holistic culture, the mind and the body are seen as one entity. Over time, the overload of external information numbs us so much that we can't carve time for our mind and body as a unit.

Build a relationship with your body. It's your soulmate and truest companion on this journey of your life, and it deserves your utmost love and attention. Like our body needs nutritious food, our mind also needs care. If both aren't aligned, that is when an imbalance occurs. Our mind needs rest, stimulation, and nutritious affirmations. For stimulating our mind, our body asks for escapes to feel that high. That high is felt when every worry has been set aside and the mind is just in the moment. Mother earth has some natural escapes that can give that high that our body and mind want, but the after effect isn't so satisfying because body did not earn that feel-good feeling. Meditating, working out, sweating through every cell after a disciplined routine can replicate those highs of life and the fruits of labour are always sweeter. Working out is not only a way for the body to let go of the weaker cells, but also give way for newer ones to grow. It is also a form of meditation because one must be present and truly be aware of each muscle they are stretching and working on. Stretching those muscles makes way for the trapped negativity to escape. People tend to quit before they even start a commitment toward their bodies, but it is an everyday habit that defines who we are.

Due to social media, the world is very aware of wise words and advice coming from many voices, but it might not work in practice. Knowing isn't enough; we have to train our minds to rewire our attitude toward life and others. It is important for our mind to observe what is around us and what we are experiencing, then take ownership of it. We might be going through certain adversities, and if we feed our mind the right thoughts by reading, observing, and internal processing instead of external, we can get through them.

The only thing that is truly in our control is our thoughts. Ultimately, even our body isn't in our control; we can't prevent its biological evolution. But we can certainly control our minds to live this life the best way it can. Since taking care of our body starts with our mind, we must build a positive relationship with food so that it reacts positively in our bodily system.

We all work and earn money to feed ourselves and our families. Sometimes, we forget to give thanks to the food we eat and the water we drink before consuming it. The simple act of saying thank you to nature and the farmers who worked so hard can help us build a positive relationship with food. It allows us to recognize the importance of what we are all living for and what sustains our life. When we put positively energized food in our body, the ailments within start to disappear.

What You Shall Sow, So Shall You Reap

Our body will feel the consequences of the junk food we eat; it will be bloated, gassy, and stressed out. However, our body will be flexible, healthy, and a supporter of our dreams if it's fed healthy food. Similarly, it is solely us who will face the consequences of our thoughts. No matter how healthy you eat, till your organs inside aren't working, it will reduce itself to waste.

Thoughts are the food for the mind, and it is solely us who will feel the consequence of whatever we feed it. If we are making excuses or victimizing ourselves for not feeling good, we are not the victim but the offender. If you are in a dark place, close your eyes, visualize the sun rising, take a deep breath, and think about how you *want* to feel in this very moment. Feel it and allow it to take over, as simple as that. We have the full-fledged ability to feel what we choose to feel.

Don't undermine the power of little attitude shifts and deep breaths.

Don't assume everyone's life is easy and without challenges. Everyone has to face challenges in life, and you can overcome those challenges with ease if you prepare your mind and body. Whenever our body has to protect itself against something foreign like an infection, our immune system automatically starts fighting the battle. Our mind needs an immunity system as well, and it is our daily habits that become our mind's defence. Meanwhile, our body is fighting so many battles that we don't even know about. We owe our body gratitude every single day because it is our companion that unconditionally loves us, even in our darkest hours.

Let Go

Every day we let go of waste from our body. We can't be at ease and go ahead with our day until we do our bathroom business. Similarly, our mind produces a lot of nonsense that is waste. We have thoughts that constipate us mentally or make us sick with stress and anxiety. We must also purge our negative thoughts every day in the form of meditation, serenading our breath, which is simply witnessing what is and letting go of what isn't.

Physical exercise, occupying our mind with hobbies, not repeating unfortunate incidents in our minds, and taking the high road are little acts of purging negativity, self-love, and a way to keep one's mind healthy. The mind and body should be fed love, which filters out into our outlook toward life. Love is a universally accepted gratifying emotion, and we must learn how to love from nature. Our body and mind, our primary companions, need and deserve our love and attention to thrive. The healthier the mind is, the healthier the body will be and vice versa.

Appreciate and take care of what you have been given so you can be deserving of more.

Chapter Six

Confidence

"All you need in this life is ignorance and confidence, and then success is sure."—Mark Twain

We meet people and come across situations every day that test our ease of being. It can be intimidating to talk to people who overpower us with their loudness, sense of entitlement, or are external processors. While some people consider it confidence, it can also be called being obnoxious.

Like happiness, confidence is another misunderstood word in our vocabulary. We have heard the phrase ignorance is bliss, but does that mean not having opinions? Must we be completely detached and turn the other cheek? Does it mean to act cocky? Does it mean to not pay heed to people or conversations that bother us? The answer is No. It can simply mean avoiding the avoidable. Avoid paying attention to words that are intentionally maligned or were spoken by someone who doesn't really know you. Avoid unnecessary confrontation with people who don't respect your individuality or have the ability to be compassionate. Avoid hanging out with people who try to provoke inferiority or flaunt their superiority. Avoid undermining your abilities and putting yourself down; it only sabotages your confidence.

Avoiding the Avoidable

> "All things truly wicked start from innocence."
> —Ernest Hemingway

Do your best to avoid gossip and don't pay attention to what others say about you from a third person. If they can't say it to your face, they probably just wanted to put you down to make themselves feel better or needed something to talk about to make their lives look interesting. The obsessive need to have the last word or sound smarter than someone else is uncalled for. There will always be someone smarter and wiser than you, and if that is possible, then there will always be someone less smart and less wise than you. Admitting that fact is the first step in taking the high road to life.

Gossiping is a distraction from focusing on who we are and what we should be paying attention to. If the mojo of our life is spent figuring out the thoughts of others, then it is an absolute waste because we are surrendering to some idealistic way of being that does not exist. Have compassion toward such occurrences instead of absorbing it in your DNA and getting consumed by the sheer futility of it. It doesn't have any purpose, goal, or meaning. It's just a waste of time and your ever-compromised mental energy. Avoiding the avoidable starts externally at first, then eventually seeps in and becomes an internal habit that leads us not to decode what others think.

The culture of "knowing it all" is a significant hindrance to becoming a compassionate and humble human. Acknowledgement that you don't have to be the smartest, brightest, or most special person in the room opens up the possibility of objectivity. For example, if someone instigates a dialogue about God in a social gathering, the contrasting opinions will pour in. They'll be immensely overwhelming to select, absorb, comprehend, criticize, and conclude in that situation. It's best to listen to the arguments from a space of detachment. Maybe we will end up learning a thing or two. But if someone says something that does not resonate with us, we can maintain a sense of detachment so our subconscious mind won't absorb the opinions that may produce distracting thoughts for us later. Ideally, we should use our minds for our own learnings, imagination, and creativity.

Job Interviews

In preparation for a job interview, people always advised me to be confident, but I could never understand what that meant. I thought I was confident every time I interviewed for a job, but I kept not hearing back from those employers. That further impacted my confidence and made me feel like I was not good enough or that I wasn't worth anything in the job market.

I must have applied for five hundred jobs, out of which I gave five or six interviews and received no positive responses. At the time, I knew that I didn't want to spend my life working at a corporate job. I wanted flexibility and to stay away from office politics and sycophancy. However, I still gained some certifications that could help me appear more skilled to a corporate employer. Still, I wasn't getting any jobs, which stripped me of any self-respect that I had for my skills. It made me feel like an utter loser.

When I finally did get hired at a job for a below-average salary, I could see my dream of owning a house or financially helping my family disappear right in front of my eyes. Then, during the COVID-19 pandemic and other vague reasons, I got let go from that job and was left with limited options. I examined what I was good at, and I landed on cooking. During years of being thrifty, I learned to cook my own food. Even though it's not a rare skill to possess, I started my own vegetarian meal delivery service. Within two months,

I had doubled the original income that I was earning while working for someone else.

I had a very successful friend in a leadership position in a very reputed firm. She made good money, but it was at the cost of her health. She ate take-out for three meals a day, plus coffee in the morning that someone else always made, and she could never truly enjoy it. In the pursuit of success at this job, her health was immensely neglected, and so was her mental state. It's like she had become her own laptop and was being controlled by others. Seeing her like that made me recognize all the positives of not working in the corporate environment. I had time for myself, my body, and my mind. More importantly, it made me realize why I was not getting hired after job interviews. I desperately tried to be someone I was not, and I wanted to give answers that appealed to others but were not authentic to who I was, so no wonder my confidence came across as a lie. The reason we get nervous is because we put ourselves down or undermine ourselves since we somewhere believe that others are better than us. Obviously, people are better than us but that does not mean that we are any less.

I felt nervous before job interviews because a boring job is not what I really wanted to do; plus, how can someone really tell what you have to offer in a thirty-minute conversation? My inner self did not align with the words that came out of my mouth. My heart wanted to be creative, and that is what I was consistently drawn to. I needed to be who I was and do what I can do best—cook and write out my thoughts. There's nothing wrong with office jobs, but many corporations overlook the interests of their employees. We need better laws that focus on the management of corporations and their responsibility toward our planet and their employees. Oh, and the managers or bosses, whatever people call them, are similar to the bouncers at a club. Their name should actually be power trips. I simply do not understand why most bosses are delusional with the power they have for the eight hours of the day that should also be assessed to make the environment at work more inclusive for all employees. The titles at work, in reality, mean nothing unless you are a prime minister or a president of a country.

I drifted away from earning my source of income from just a job and started focusing on what I was capable of within my own devices. The moment I focused on what I wanted to do; I was at peace. It lifted the veil of stress from my mind, and I was able to live freely. All it took was recognition of who I really was and who I was not comfortable being. Pretending to be someone else doesn't only drain you, but the people around you will catch on eventually. The energies that rule us will catch on as well, and then we will only attract people who are pretending to be someone else too.

I realized I sucked at job interviews because, first, I don't believe in what I was interviewing for or care enough for it and second, I felt intimidated because I did not add any productivity into my life for myself.

Don't be so hard on yourself for not being confident at times in situations where you are supposed to shine. Inject some productivity into your life, derive your own self-worth, and keep going. I just did that because no one was interested in hiring me. When I wasn't even looking for a job, I got a call out of the blue from a company whose ideology I aligned with. They hired me and that made me realize what is meant for you will be yours and what is not meant for you will never be yours, no matter how hard you try.

Know Thyself

Innocence stems from ignorance, and an innocent face is the most beautiful face ever. Having a non-indulgent approach to the aspects of life that make you bitter will cause you to focus on what you have now. The more you refrain from diving into conspicuous matters, the more your energy will be diverted toward yourself. The more your cup within is full, the more it will runneth over.

The more aspects you know about yourself, the more you'll know what areas of your life you should spend your energy on. For example, if people get peer pressured into posting a picture for a cause on their social media accounts without doing proper research first, it can distract from the cause itself. Our social media posts aren't a political petition, and the people suffering aren't checking out the hashtag to heal their pains. It is merely a distraction from the real issues. The real issues are infrastructure in developing countries, corruption, misuse of democracy, overfishing, et cetera, and only people in power with money control the majority of decision making. The COVID-19 pandemic showed us how big box stores were considered essential; meanwhile, a small restaurant was deemed unessential. Schools were shut, whereas rallies for votes were allowed. To make a change, we must first make ourselves capable and to be capable, a step forward in our own personal behaviours and attitudes must occur. Our decision of how we want to live in this world matters the most in creating our reality. It has also become difficult to know what the truth and logic are in any of the information we come across. Sometimes, the reality is not as bad as we make it. Sadly, this is the world we live in; a little twisted. But a smile is contagious.

Praying and sending positive vibes to people who are sincerely suffering may uplift their souls, but how can we do that if we spend our energy wanting to appear sensitive instead of compassionately feeling the grief? In our current circumstances of information pollution, it is time to step back and focus on our lives a bit more. The best way to be kinder is to first be kind to yourself and then to the people around you. Help the ones who are around and need it the most. Refrain from many frustrations as a result of social media.

The more you know yourself, the more you will be faithful to your life and won't need anyone's validation to direct your intentions and actions. Preserving your energy for self-awareness will only help you become stronger and closer with yourself. It will be harder for other people to break your spirit or to manipulate you into doing or believing something that does not align with you.

Our relationship with ourselves is contingent on what we focus our energy on. If we are depleting all our energy in front of a screen, then we will have no imagination or creativity of our own. We've spent all our time being manipulated by an overload of information coming through the screen.

If our focus is on other people, then we are just narrating a story with a cast of those people. If our focus is on possessions, then remember that everything we pour our money into is leased until our life is over. You can't get out of debt without paying a penalty, and eventually, you are liable for that debt. The more we hold, the more we weigh. The more we focus on outer attachments, the further we will be from our inner selves. The closer we are to ourselves only then can we become familiar with our strengths and weaknesses. As we grow our familiarity with ourselves, the easier it becomes to control our minds.

A few minutes of reflection each day can remind us that with each passing hour, we are changing, so to be in touch with ourselves is immensely important. It is important to shut off the energy-sucking thinking part of the brain and be truly present in the moment to enjoy life and the task at hand. Confidence is not permanent; it's through a daily practice of self-recognition that we gain this ability. Delusion arises when there is no alignment between our actions and our words. The more we focus on what we are saying, the less it will matter what others want us to say and do. Being sure of who we are and what we can bring to the table, even if it's just an ear to listen with, is the greatest authenticity we can have.

Know thyself. As humans, we have so many qualities that we can feel good about, like not taking no for an answer and always being willing to find a way to resolve just about everything, being adaptable, having awareness to actively focus on what is rather than what is not and being able to motivate oneself by seeking knowledge. If we have a strong relationship with our best qualities, then we will never be shy of confidence.

Be Aware of Your Ego

"When ego is lost, limit is lost. You become infinite, kind, beautiful." —Yogi Bhajan

Our ego is afraid of dying because many people only identify themselves based on their possessions and other things outside of themselves. The fear of losing everything material is created by our ego. An egoistic person believes that the earth revolves around them. However, time does not stop for anyone. When life passes by without any fruitful progress, one can suddenly wake up at the age of forty-five feeling miserable, depressed, and jaded. I've seen that happen a lot.

Our ego distances us from ourselves. When we forget that everyone is equally special, everyone has the same fate, and everyone desires excellence for themselves, then we are building our beliefs on a fractured foundation. Our theories and ideas will be proven false if they are not authentic to the reality of life. No matter how amazing of a businessman you are, there will always be someone who is better than you. No matter how perfect the weather on a summer night by the beach is, there always be a place with better weather and a prettier view. If we maintain a lack of this awareness, then that makes us an egoistic snob. We'll overestimate our strengths and block ourselves from growing beyond what we know.

When our thoughts and actions arise from the notion that "I'm the most special person," then our only pursuits will be to be liked and be better than others. What is that type of life revolving around? It's living in comparison to others, which means it's not entirely yours. A life that is lived to feel better, by comparison, will only give rise to jealousy and competitiveness and will also make you constantly look for your own shortcomings. Having those emotions inside is like smoking twenty cigarettes a day. Even if there is fresh oxygen in our environment, we deliberately breathe in chemicals to harm our lungs.

A confident person is aware that they are not special; they are just a human, here to learn and grow. Their pursuit becomes one of excellence and advancement to higher limits, leading them to live their best lives. Knowing that life is a classroom, and we are solely responsible for our thoughts and actions spawns our trust to focus on greatness.

If you are sure that two plus two is four, you won't need to enforce that logic on anyone. Similarly, if you are sure of who you are, you won't need to enforce your views or ways on anyone else. You are not living their life since you are already busy living yours. That allows other people to be their genuine selves around you. If you can conquer yourself, that is the biggest badge of honour. Discipline, self-control, consistency, and determination all rise from a belief that "I am only human. I need to work hard, control where I focus my energy, and live my best self." It is the best way to instill confidence in oneself. Confidence isn't being proud, it isn't being happy with yourself, and it isn't a complicated behaviour. It is simply an awareness that we are not above anyone, and no one is above us. Only you are a contributor to your confidence, and it comes from earning that for yourself by keeping busy with productive and unproductive things.

Don't let someone else's idea of confidence ruin your version of it. Life is too short to worry about what others think. They aren't paying your bills or digesting the food you eat. Becoming someone else defeats who you are. Have good intentions, be a part of this universe, and do not let others live for free in your head. Confidence comes when you learn something productive. It's a result of knowing who you are and that no one can validate you but yourself.

Confidence isn't loud or being conceited because when you won't be recognized, it will hurt. It is knowing when to speak and when not to. It is deciding where to spend your energy and where not to. It is contentment and acceptance of this human form. Confidence comes when we live in the moment and recognize all the moments before when thousands of cells inside of us died while many new ones were born. Confidence is a smile that we put on in exchange for a breath from nature. It is eloquent words that reflect the beauty in this world and are not pretentious. It just is being perfectly okay with who you are in this very moment. Humbleness is true confidence because you do not need anyone else to validate your ideas, or sharpen your inner grace; it has a way of attracting success. Do not be deluged by negative self-beliefs. You are the one that needs to empower yourself. Find something amazing within you and make it count.

Focusing on my abilities made me confident and made me okay in my own skin. I felt fulfilled because I had learned that my fate is not in anyone's hand, but it is dependent entirely on my thoughts and point of view. I didn't need validation or acceptance because even the aimless birds and plucky spiders were being fed by the universe, so I was sure that there was a bigger scheme at work here. What was meant to be would be mine and it was first my responsibility to attune myself to my uniqueness, which were my experiences and abilities by writing this book! We all have a unique bug within us and if we submerge it with our perceptions of others, then that poor li'l fella ought to disappear.

Chapter Seven

Communication

"Wise men talk because they have something to say; fools, because they would like to say something." —Plato

Communication is so vital that educational institutes have an entire field of study on the subject. Often, if we don't recognize how and what we are communicating, it can cause a ripple effect in our lives. How are relationships and friendships primarily built? It's through positive communication and the ability to speak freely to communicate your feelings. A person who cannot speak, using their voice or otherwise, will have a difficult time maintaining relationships. This is another thing we take for granted: the ability to speak.

Some professional motivational speakers uplift the spirits of massive audiences. Political and business leaders can hypnotize an entire arena by using their speeches filled with enthusiasm. The way an actor delivers a performance can make or break their career, and how one communicates in a job interview can decide their livelihood. The way we communicate holds so much power in how we can control the situation and our environment.

Listening

No one wants you to solve their problems for them unless they ask for it. When conversing with certain individuals, it can be really draining because all they do is grumble. In those moments, we urge to resolve their problems and I am a culprit of that myself. It's some people's habit to find problems with every solution and more often or not, they do not end up resolving anything but confusing themselves. Others want to simply create problems in their lives because they can't digest their beautiful lives. When we butt in, in their own internal conflicts, we do nothing but take over their thoughts and problems onto ourselves and why is that? It is because they are not listening, so it bounces back. It is like throwing a ball at a wall. Those difficult people want to just be validated and heard because they themselves cannot process their wandering thoughts and mind. In those situations, like my dad recommends, either change the subject, get busy, or just let them vent and consider yourself a charitable unpaid therapist; in a way, you are doing a charity by donating your hearing abilities. Hear but, don't listen. I really love and hate this quality of my husband; he is always hearing and at the same time, zoned out in his la la land.

My niece, who is three years old, was very flustered one day when she was asked to pack up her toys and eat her lunch. She fought with adults to let her play with her toys instead of doing anything else. Then I saw my sister-in-law, her momma, politely explaining to her the logic behind why she should eat her lunch so she can feel energized, and resume playing and not feel tired afterwards. My niece understood and that just blew my mind! How much approaching a situation by bringing in the idea of thinking logically can enforce productive results! Assuming that other people already know and understand what we are feeling, or thinking is what creates conflicts in the first place. Letting people logically understand our needs requires patience and effort, just like everything in life!

We all have heard the infamous phrase, "think before you speak," but what does that really imply? Do we need to always filter ourselves? Yes, it does. That moment you take to think before speaking, especially in a difficult or frustrating situation, can be absolutely worth it. Some battles are best to be avoided. Preventing ourselves from continuing to communicate with a person who has their own internal miscommunication can save us a lot of energy. When someone utters or does anything that does not serve us, we instantly get angry. We justify our anger in our head and then exhale fire at people or at least want to. When one gets angry, one's body is the primal receiver of it. Anger activates the amygdala (collections of cells in the base of the brain, where our emotions are interpreted), which further activates the hypothalamus that transfers the information to our pituitary gland by releasing a hormone. The gland then awakens our adrenal glands, which release stress-induced hormones into our body. It increases our heart rate, blood pressure, acid level, et cetera. After our body, it affects our mind to lose control over our communication with others, ultimately affecting our relationship(s). In some connections of life, we need to be a bit more patient, respectful, and logical. When a conversation gets difficult, it is imperative to bring in the idea of applying logic or encouraging the other person to be logical by guiding them because at times we tend to get sidetracked and get caught up with our emotions.

I am myself a culprit of lashing out at people and I hope in their hearts they can find the strength to forgive me. We all can relay our frustrations, fears, anger, and disappointment with our ability to patiently speak. It is important to stop and listen to ourselves while uttering our words. When we both talk and listen to ourselves, we're able to judge our minds and our priorities. If we just talk without listening, then it's not a conversation; it is the drums of our insecurities beating. We should listen to ourselves and really hear what we are trying to convey. Would we like to listen to the mindless chatter coming out of our mouths? Is it inviting to the other person? Is it uplifting anyone's spirits? Listening to ourselves might address some of these questions.

Some of us haven't sharpened our ability to listen, which has prevented us from understanding how our relationships have gone wrong. Why do couples end up in heart-wrenching conflicts? It's because when emotions take over our ability to communicate, all our logic and sense flow down the drain when faced with conflict. We should be cautious about how we speak to the people closest to us. It literally defines how we want to be loved.

Communication isn't only what we speak, but also what we don't speak. I realized the importance of communication when I first witnessed my parents' bicker with each other for no reason. They are a wonderful couple, but sometimes my father's baby-like repetitive questions would get under my mother's skin. She'd snap at him, and in return, my dad would throw a tantrum. That would agitate her, and the cycle would continue until it became the normal way they'd communicate.

Many marital relationships include bouts of bickering, even if the relationship appears flawless on social media. This is just one of the examples of how miscommunication can cause a divide between people. A smile on the face is also a way to communicate; it is how we show each other what we have running inside of us.

Communication includes speaking from our mouth and listening from our ears. The words that come out of us are created from within, which implies the digestion of our thoughts happens inside of us and how we choose to digest the information we absorb is based on how we have tuned our filters.

Self-Communication

> "A man's character may be learned from the adjectives which he habitually uses in conversation." — Mark Twain

The most important communication is our communication with ourselves. What we put inside of us in every moment is what creates our reality. Water hydrates us, and alcohol dehydrates us. They are both liquids, bring pleasure, and quench our thirst, but they do very different things inside our bodies. We are constantly communicating with ourselves and what we send out to the world, and we are not even aware of it.

If we have grand intentions, goals, motives, or dreams, yet we confuse our body with negative thoughts like "it's impossible," our actions do not align with our desires. It is bound to become an internal mess, followed by feeling lost externally. To cook a delicious meal, one must understand its ingredients and know how much is required for the perfect taste. If we aren't accustomed to the ingredients, then the meal might end up disastrous. What we communicate to ourselves is the meal we are preparing for us to relish.

Just as we are expected to be gentle in our communication with others, we must first begin that practice with ourselves. It's not good enough to settle for the frustrated phrases we keep uttering to ourselves. The moment we say something negative about ourselves out loud, it becomes a part of us. We make ourselves believe that it is okay to be negative because we have valid reasons, but this makes our body and subconscious mind seek reasons to feel jaded.

It's essential to effectively communicate goals and strategies to climb the ladder to success in a corporate work environment. Communication is how problems and urgencies are relayed, how solutions are strategized, and how accountability is addressed. To be a great leader or an effective team player, it is important to be objective rather than subjective toward our peers and to communicate in a pleasant and socially acceptable manner even if the other person does not deserve it. Having good qualities has a way of being recognized, whether instantly or in the distant future.

In our personal lives, we tend to let go of our goal to coexist happily ever after. Instead, we become subjective toward the people we live with. We start nit-picking or putting others down because our short-term goal is to feel better by blaming our discontent on someone else. This wouldn't last in a job, so it certainly wouldn't last in our personal lives. We must communicate sensibly with the people we spend the most time with, and with ourselves, because our words have an effect.

Being a difficult communicator, getting instantly agitated, having an irritable personality, or not respecting another human's existence can significantly sabotage a relationship's growth. Politeness goes a long way, and it allows others around us to feel comfortable. This only makes our bond stronger. If happiness resides in our homes, that happiness will radiate from us outside of our homes. If you're nice to others while being a pain in the ass to your family members, it'll be evident to your wider network as well.

Select *Who you Converse With*

> "Who you are speaks so loudly I can't hear what you're saying." —Ralph Waldo Emerson

It is up to us to improve our relationships by adjusting the way we communicate based on people's different personalities. If we've tried everything and someone is still difficult to communicate with, then there is no reason to continue carrying on a sensible conversation. No matter what we say, they will not hear us because they are so blocked off by their own miscommunication. It is best to reverse your engines, detach, conserve your energy, and zone out in those scenarios. Let people absorb their own mess and do not act in their theatre. They don't need you to save them.

Sometimes, it's necessary to let go and shield yourself from conversations that are depleting. It is not our job to fix everyone, but it is our job to protect ourselves from what we consume. We don't have to win every battle. Instead, we should be selective in the battles we pick. It is not worth fighting with someone weaker than us, and it is definitely not worth fighting with someone stronger than us. Sometimes even the most difficult people can teach us a thing or two, and if we can extract their beautiful qualities, then we have won regardless.

I used to have a hard time with a know-it-all coworker who sat right next to me. She would always add her two cents on every subject and had a terrible habit of butting in on peoples' conversations; she was an external processor. Sometimes, her attitude would come across as condescending, obnoxious, and annoying. Even if something wasn't about her, she would make it about herself. She did not seem like a person I would like to have a glass of wine with. I would dread going to work and seeing her on the days I was PMS-ing. Sometimes, I thought I might just snap to shut her up.

I struggled for a year to find ways to tolerate her. Then, one day I noticed she was in a foul mood. It was making her even more miserable, as though she was defeated by life. She had an internal battle to make sense of her own life because she always needed validation and wanted to be noticed. A person who is really at peace and in alignment with their mind and soul does not need anyone else's opinion or approval. It's like she hoped for an opinion back so she could defy it and feel better about herself. We all have managers at work who are on an ego trip like the bouncers of a busy club. Damn! Is it every hard to be in a situation when one cannot speak up against their bosses who are maligned and not good leaders. The only lesson I have learnt being in that situation is that you cannot really change anyone, but the only thing you can change is your environment. Sometimes, it is absolutely necessary to leave a bitter situation and create a better situation for oneself like everything else in life and for the managers…life eventually catches up. Patience is also a way of communicating to the universe to let it do its thing of what goes around, comes around.

In that moment, I empathized with her. It became easier for me to communicate with her. I realized that whatever she uttered wasn't targeted toward me. It was her own battle within. I don't know exactly what was going on, but it was not my problem. I can't add people's miseries to my own. However, I respected her internal battle, and I asked myself, why did she bother me in the first place? It was because there was a part of me that also wanted to be validated, liked, and respected. I expected her to be exactly the way I like. A person who imposes their views on others does so because they aren't sure of their view of themselves. They want other people to walk with them on their path, so they are not alone.

If we have been given the blessing of speaking, then we must use it wisely and be mindful of how we talk with one another.

At a psychologist's clinic, a person is first just advised to talk freely without hesitating and let their true insights flow out. This helps the psychologist gauge what a person's inner truest thoughts and concerns are. Sometimes, when we speak without thinking, we give power to the other person to decipher who we are.

Choose Your Words Carefully

"As empty vessels make the loudest sound, so they that have the least wit are the greatest blabbers." —Plato

When we become aware of what we wouldn't like being done to us, we won't turn around and do those things to others. We understand that it will make the other person uncomfortable and can see that it may ruin our relationship. Frankly, that outcome is such a burden. Living with this awareness will bring us challenges that force us to learn about life. I believe when I leave this earth, I don't want to carry any baggage filled with resentments or grudges. One way or the other, we have to learn to let go of everything that ties us consciously and subconsciously. It is creating extra unnecessary luggage in our minds.

Our words can hold immense power over others, sometimes knowingly and other times unknowingly. What we say to people outside of us can stay with them forever. We don't want to be a villain in anyone else's life, so we should be mindful of what we say

121

to others and how we communicate, both verbally and physically.

Nobody appreciates a mean spirit; it only pushes people away. Whatever we communicate on a day-to-day basis with others should be pleasant for anyone to absorb. It is not just about us in this world. If that were the case, we would not be social beings. All relationships are built and sustained on our ability to communicate lovingly. A cake is decorated with frosting and fruits to make it more appetizing. It could be the most delicious cake inside, but it will seem inedible if it is decorated with spicy peppers. Even truth needs to be wrapped nicely in the way it's communicated, or it will lose its significance.

When people consistently disappoint, it's not their fault. It's our fault because we forget that they are simply not aware. It is like expecting a scorpion to not sting. The best way to communicate with unaware folks is to detach yourself from playing their games. Communication should not be contingent on how others talk to us. We should always allow a way to let the best version of us shine.

Whatever and however we utter something, it becomes our reality. Every time we take the high road, it's an act of self-love. It is not for them; it is for us. Certain situations, especially the most vulnerable ones, are truly the test of who we are and not who others are. It takes effort and maturity to be in control of your emotions, unlike a child, who has no control.

We often forget that there's a fine line between what we are communicating versus who we are. Sometimes we relay the sheer opposite of who we really are. For instance, some people want to solve a problem, but their emotions take over. Instead of figuring out a problem or feeling, they just end up relaying their frustration, making communication difficult and limited. In the end, we are the beneficiaries of our actions. Bad or good, it is ours to deal with.

Communicate

Differences arise when we do not describe our true feelings to others. It is not the job of others to constantly figure out what the other is feeling. If we have a conflict with someone, it is important to effectively communicate our thoughts and not attach aggressively passionate emotion to it because the content of the matter can get subdued or lost in the loudness. Many times, people hesitate to effectively communicate how they are feeling, which leads to thoughts forming deep knots inside. Because we do not iron out any conflicts at the onset, we end up building a whole mountain of complexes within us which further impacts our relationships with others. If a path of silence is chosen, then it is important to comprehend why that road was chosen and then match the silence on the inside to the silence on the outside. Leaving for others to guess our unspoken words is burdening the other person and it is shrugging away the responsibility to maintain a relationship.

The words we utter display our intentions and true character. It's up to us to have control over what, how, and to whom we say what we want to say. Ultimately, we are only responsible for what we say, not what others understand. They will understand based on their level of cognitive ability and mental capability. Water throughout the world is collected from the same sources—rains, dams, rivers, or lakes—but it is dependent on the individual filtration systems of each city to manage how that water is treated for consumption.

It is our responsibility to change the flow of energy in every person we communicate with. Our thoughts are the signals we send to our body, and our tongue is the radio. We can tune our thoughts to the right frequency, so we play good melodies through our radios. A soft melody can heal a broken heart, and upbeat music can turn up a party. Our words are always followed by a rhythm, and that rhythm comes from the tunes that are playing inside us. Everyone appreciates a good sound, and there is nothing worse than the sound of an untuned instrument.

The best use of our mouth is when we can utter something that will make the ones around us laugh; it is not only an excellent quality that attracts people, but is also the most intelligent attribute one can possess within. We cannot always help others monetarily or emotionally but laughing helps the flow of blood and that is the easiest way to do our bit to uplift others.

One fine early morning, I was chilling on my balcony, sipping my cup of coffee. I was hypnotically lost in the beautiful sound of birds chirping while the world was waking up. Suddenly, a crow stood on the railing and started cawing so loudly that I had to get up and go inside. Let's not be crows. Let's be the beautiful chirpy birds who bring peace to the souls of others and make everyone around us dance to the tunes we play.

Chapter Eight

Spirit

"Science is the acceptance of what works and the rejection of what does not. That needs more courage than what we might think." —*Jacob Bronowski*

The most vital ingredient to our life is the air that we breathe in and breathe out. It's a metaphor; what keeps us surviving is something that we cannot see. Our human make-up does not consist of our mind, body, and then soul, but it's our soul within our mind and body. Though we only have one body, we have many minds.

People often confuse spirituality with religion. Religion is a practice, a language in which one prays or from which one derives fulfillment of their devotion toward the unknown. Spirituality is being aware of the invisible forces that govern our life. Humans cannot see spirits or talk to their souls, so little emphasis is placed on it. It remains invisible, like the air we breathe, so no wonder we keep on polluting our spiritual environment.

If you have ever seen a dead body, it feels as though something that made them alive left their body. They become just a piece of mass. The very life we have is our spirit, and yet most of us are far from embracing the spiritual life within us.

It is very difficult to connect with one's core these days because of our digital devices. I am myself a victim of it. Out of twenty-four hours in a day, we sleep on average for eight, work and travel for ten, run our errands for a minimum of four, and spend two hours on miscellaneous activities. In the background, we focus on our devices. We stare at wise words online but never implement them. Most people I meet are aware of wonderful sayings and teachings, but I rarely come across people who actively practice what they preach. How you are breathing reflects how healthy your lungs are, your physical energy reflects how healthy your body is, and the thoughts that keep springing in your head are a mirror to how your spirit is. Many times, we keep circulating information and details about our past or others, and that speaks volumes of where we are in our journey of life. We don't need an expert astrologer to make us aware of our challenges or a past life regression therapy; we ourselves can be our fortune tellers if we tune ourselves to find our shortcomings, which are inhibiting us from living an unchained life. By intro-specting what we keep circulating within us, we can maybe become our own psychics.

What we Can (and Cannot) Control

We become control freaks because we cannot see our soul or the laws and energies governing the universe. We take matters into our own hands, thinking that it is all up to us, but it isn't. When we realize what we cannot control, we lose our balance and convic-tion of the higher truths that we want to believe in. In Hinduism, there is a divine employee of God named Chitra (character) gupt (unexposed/secret), or Chitragupta, who keeps a log of each moment of our life; our intentions, deeds, thoughts, and even the food we eat. Accordingly, Chitragupta assigns us a life that we deserve.

The primary law of physics states that every action has an equal and opposite reaction, which in philosophy is known as *karma*. What goes around comes around. Just because we cannot see an imme-diate result, we may think that all the laws are futile and what we do, say, and think has no significance. Hoarding materials, turning people against each other, considering ourselves superior, extracting wealth out of others, trying to outsmart others, being inconsiderate, talking rudely to people, not counting one's blessings, being condescending, or making up stories about others are some of the attributes of people who think they're temporarily controlling their lives. However, all those actions are being noted somewhere, maybe up in the sky, maybe within your soul, or maybe down in hell. We then ask the infamous question, "Why did this happen to me?"

It is hard for us to take responsibility for our own existence and even harder to understand our spirit's journey and extract meaning from it. The misunderstanding or missed lessons from an event become our baggage, especially when we do not derive a lesson from an uncomfortable situation. We all are carrying baggage from our past lives. The only way to get rid of that weight is to stop, unload, and discard what is not serving us. Any thoughts that give us a limited mindset should be discarded if we want to move forward freely because if we are walking forward while looking backward, then we are bound to bump into something ahead.

It's also important to recognize the fact that nobody is perfect, and we all make mistakes. We all have to face certain setbacks in life, and the moment we realize that and understand that we have the power not to repeat the bad things, good changes can begin. When we know better but still cannot bring that self-discipline into our lives, then we are simply fools who deserve mediocrity.

Knowing how to work out doesn't get you in shape; sweating does. Why is it so hard for us to vibrate on a higher frequency in life and let go of being control freaks? Or to not be in constant competition with others? Or just simply accept and love everyone, including ourselves? It's because we think we are in control, and we forget that there are deeper, scientific, and chaotically organized forces we live with that are beyond our immediate understanding.

Give Your Soul Space

We have limitations on our memory. While going to bed or waking up early in the morning, we know there is a system at play. There will be dawn and dusk. Birds sleep at night and wake the world up with their chirping in the morning. The sun will rise, the rooster will crow, the earth will revolve and rotate, the moon will wane. Clouds will form, rain will pour, and evaporation will follow. Everything is in order; everything works based on the laws of nature.

Humans are a result of years of evolution. We learned to decode scientific techniques that advanced our species. Scientists who research for decades use trial and error with patience, which has allowed them to formulate theses and draw conclusions. These are the paradigms of our current world and how we humans inhabitant our planet.

If certain laws govern everything, then our soul is no exception. Our soul or spirit that gives us a temporary human life is constantly evolving with our experiences, thoughts, and vibrations we create within. We are constantly playing a part in the larger scheme of things, and because we do not constantly see things tangibly, we tend to forgo our understanding that we are only in control of our minds. The rest is science and nature doing its thing.

Social media platforms grip our attention because it constantly feeds us, which means we don't have to work our brain muscle to achieve any fulfillment. A pizza only tastes good when the dough is kneaded, tomatoes are crushed and cooked, vegetables are grown and chopped, and milk is fermented to form cheese. Together, they blend with each other in the oven to satisfy our appetite and taste palette. If I were to just put flour, yeast, salt, sugar, some seeds, and milk on top of a lighter, they couldn't possibly be served at a restaurant. Our mind needs kneading, fermenting, some cooking time, patience, and labour to really put it to use.

The person who can never be alone or by themselves is the most miserable human being on this planet because they are so far detached from who they are and are simply living mindlessly. I am sure many of us have tried to sit in silence for a few minutes and realized that our mind wanders, sometimes reliving the past and creating unnecessary friction. Or perhaps our hands have reflexively grabbed our digital devices to feed our brains with images, thoughts, or updates to create inspiration within. There is nothing new that flows, no introspection, which means no inner rewiring. We may spend our energy reading wonderful quotes, but we can never align ourselves to vibrate higher if we don't give ourselves space to absorb it. We simply end up being a captive of our ego, our ignorance, and our own trappings.

When the mind is constantly wired to be trapped by limitations, no new day will be enjoyed or lived in a new way. Change and adaptability become incredibly onerous because the mind is finite. We hold on to our jobs that we don't like because we are afraid of stepping into something new. We hold on to our behaviours because we find it difficult to change into a nicer or bigger person. It isn't serving our ego, and that attitude is carried on until relationships become tasteless, and at times, even bitter.

I used to date a guy who cheated on me, and I kept going back to him because I couldn't imagine that there was love in the world for me beyond this one man without integrity. I was trapped until I moved far away, and I was forced to spend time with myself. I realized I needed to break my habit of having no integrity myself by chasing someone who made me feel replaceable. Now that I look back at the situation, I realized it wasn't that guy who was at fault; it was me because I was trying to be a hero in someone's else story.

While going through the process of shedding my feelings for someone like that, I grew closer to myself and realized I needed to love myself first by doing things that make me feel good. Dancing, watching a good flick, drinking wine, cleaning, reading, cooking, meditating, and so many other awesome things that made me live to the fullest, instead of moping around in my bedroom, bitching about people who made me feel insecure.

Whenever I've watched horrific crime stories, it's made me wonder why some people are so lawless, immoral, and full of extreme anger. A common confession of criminals is that they had no idea how their extreme rage took over. They did not believe they could commit something like that. They were ruled by something in the moment that was more powerful than their own mind, which resulted in time spent in a dark prison, or worse. When people have absolutely no connection to their mind, spirit, and the laws of nature, that is when they start messing with the divinity of existence. It always starts with small incidents that grow with such intensity that one exudes extreme behaviours. We all are instigators of small behaviours that eventually grow into our biggest problems.

Surrender to the Moment

It is essential to breathe deeply and meditate, or in other words, witness the moment we are existing in. It not only scientifically relaxes the mind but also gives us greater self-control over our emotions. Consider how everything is so mathematical these days, with coding, algorithms, data, et cetera. We all should have a log of our daily happiness, mood, and behaviour rating so we can keep a tally of how often we get manipulated by things outside of us instead of administrating our own lives. Maybe that will make it clear who we are and where changes need to happen.

Instead of controlling our minds, we tend to focus on controlling every other insignificant detail, which creates hurdles for us to practice detachment and patience. A person who is in close contact with themselves is confident that they can control their mind, and life is working in collaboration with nature and science. A person who is detached from who they are will always find unhappiness, anxiety, and a controlling ego.

Anger is the most deteriorating emotion one can feel. It's created out of judgment, expectation, ego, self-serving bias, and even has a direct effect on our breathing. Anger clouds our judgment of a situation, impairs our speech, and causes a chain effect on the mind and body that pushes us further from ourselves. With meditation, we can learn to prevent these bouts of anger by controlling our egos.

If you always find yourself thinking about others or about what they said or did, then you are filling yourself with thoughts that create ego. Thoughts of what others do versus what you would do. Our ego causes us to indulge in two things, negative tittle-tattle about others or to brag about oneself. It's like calling a rose a spine and spine a rose. Both are incorrect and unreal. Creating such unrealistic thoughts and ideas will only cause us to be delusional in life. To prevent our ego from taking over, we can use meditation to seek solace and connection within. Most of us are so full of other noises that we are alien to who we are and our power. Meditation can help us tap into that power.

Who Are We Truly?

*"We are not human beings having a spiritual experience.
We are spiritual beings having a human experience."*
—*Pierre Teilhard de Chardin*

We are at our core neither our family's last name, the house we live in, nor the job that we do. We are neither the relationships we have nor the titles we hold. We are not defined by our ethnicity and are not confined by our emotions. We are, first and foremost, a form of energy compounded into a human form.

Water, the source of life, is made of two atoms of hydrogen and one atom of oxygen. However, if you combine two atoms of hydrogen with two atoms of oxygen, it produces hydrogen peroxide, a bleaching agent that is poisonous if consumed. Our energy is compounded with other elements, like our thoughts, the words we utter, and the deeds that we do. They all come together to form the life that we deserve on this planet. At times, we are just bleaching agents in human form, but that discussion is for another time. It is our energy that chooses the life we live and the challenges we have to overcome. We must not forget that every single human on this planet has their own challenges to overcome. We are the ones who chose and formulated this life—no one else. Every experience is what we have invited.

How much of your infancy do you clearly remember? Your body carries birthmarks or forms a scar if someone dropped you as a baby. But why can't we remember any of it? With passing time, we forget what formed us, how little we once were, and how big we've grown. We were created from a minuscule egg and sperm—how magical is that?! We exist because two people were in love (or at least one person was, we hope!), and it's easy to forget that. We forget who we really are, and it's just how the nature of existence is. We start living our lives based on our ethnicities, geographies, relationships, emotions, finances, and professions first, which causes us to neglect our very core, our spirit.

We must get to know our spirit and remember it's the foundation of our life—it cannot have any cracks or, in some cases, be completely missing. We must spend time to get to know ourselves, discard what doesn't serve us, and let go or make sense of why something happened. Gracefully accepting the events that led us to today will help us move forward with the utmost conviction that you have your soul, and you need nothing else.

To fill in, first you need to shed—shed your old ways of perceiving the world, let go of what you have learned, talk to yourself, and ask yourself what is really bothering you. Why are your relationships bad, or why is your physical health always suffering? Making excuses won't suffice. It's just a matter of priorities and giving yourself solitude—with no digital devices to distract you. Just you and the air you need to breathe. Get in touch with that vast energy within you. Employ yourself as your own CEO to manage your own thoughts. Spend time with yourself; it's the biggest luxury you can ever have. There is a whole universe to be explored within you. It takes time, it takes early mornings, it takes a minute before reacting to every situation, and it takes seconds before the biggest performance. One of the greatest, easiest, and most economical ways to imbibe your solitude is by taking the dog in you for a walk. Walking is a great stimulator and also an excellent way to stay fit!

Realize that you need to serve the energy within you and not what is on the surface. You have to serve your own master within you, constantly and persistently. Then, controlling your mind becomes a habit that is learned with everyday practice. Depression, distress, stress, and emotional instability are a result of losing that control. Do not swim in the luxury of self-pity, convincing yourself that it is alright to feel that way. You do not deserve to feel grief for yourself for days. You are repeating the pattern that got you in that misery in the first place—STOP.

Soothe Your Soul

*"Despair is a narcotic. It lulls the mind
into indifference."* —Charlie Chaplin

To stave off depression, go for a walk by yourself. Also, laughter is a "must" to ease the mind. Sitting and dissolving yourself in darkness is no way to uplift your spirit. Why waste such a beautiful life? If you love and honour yourself, then why not do things that will uplift the brain?

Be present in the moment and take control of your mind.

But what do inner growth, being calm, and being a jolly-natured fellow really do? These create space within to explore the dimensions that induce high spirits and allow us to focus on possibilities that further expand who we really are or can become. We don't only uplift ourselves; we also end up uplifting those around us who are near and dear. Nothing can cause us to be high or low because we are already in alignment with our lows and highs. When the mind is at peace, uncloudy, and available for more, the opportunity knocks to find another dimension of ourselves.

Our soul is our spirit. It's the way we want to live our lives, and it requires effort to stay in high spirits. In Sikhism, this is called *Chardi Kala*, meaning to always remain in high spirits no matter what it takes. Do not let circumstances dictate how you should feel. Instead, look up, fill yourself with the fuel of oxygen, and let the trappings of a situation on your mind go.

Everything comes, and everything goes. The charm of something new fades, and sometimes It's the old things or ideas we take for granted. We may have forgotten what gives us the feeling of love and happiness. It requires effort not to forget the bigger picture and live the life that we have been given with all the good and all the bad it involves. Because ultimately, we all have the same fate. It is up to us how we steer the wheel of our inner core.

Nothing can satisfy the hunger of our soul. No food, no material, or relationship can ever quench the thirst for what the soul needs. The purpose of indulging in some form of art or connecting to the energy of the universe that governs life is to align us to our soul so it can align itself with what it's aching for. Our mind is a wandering cat. It lusts for many things, but our spirit aches for only one thing—to find its higher existence within the form it is in now. Our mind has the power to turn a blessing into a curse and a curse into a blessing. The randomness within us isn't our spirit; it is our mind that is wandering, trying to manifest its challenges. Don't let it win.

There is a reason your life manifested in you and wanted to experience what you are experiencing in this moment. It will answer how the challenges of your existence can be resolved, but only if you let it guide you. Everyone's spirit wants to be at peace, to be content, and to enjoy this human form. Sometimes, certain challenges make us unique and give us the opportunity to lead a unique life. One of the best ways to identify your own dilemmas within is to recognize how you feel and think about others. When we look into others' lives, we live outwardly. When we fall in love, we only see the best in the other person; the more we spend time with someone, the more we become aware about them. Spending energy in analyzing others isn't deep. It's an attribute of the shallow mind. To stay in love, we must remove ourselves from dissecting others. People who are aware of this accept their shortcomings within and do not focus on the shortcomings of others. Little tweaking of ourselves manifest the most rewarding experiences, which bring healing to our aching spirit.

Chapter Nine

Discipline

"You will never have a greater or lesser dominion than that over yourself . . . the height of a man's success is gauged by his self-mastery; the depth of his failure by his self-abandonment . . . and this law is the expression of eternal justice. He who cannot establish dominion over himself will have no dominion over others."
—Leonardo da Vinci

Growing up, I was never a straight-A student or master of any extracurricular activities. I found myself to be a jack of all trades. I wasted my time by watching a lot of cartoons and all the Disney shows. I participated in dance, sports, music, and drama, but visual art was never my forte. My dad used to do my art homework when I left it for the last moment so I wouldn't fail the subject. In India, academics is a competitive field, which is why every second kid grew up to be an accountant, doctor, or engineer. But I never was one of those. In fact, I used to study two to three hours before my exams just to get a passing grade. My mother always asked me if I was ever going to make her proud in academics. My answer was always, "Wait for my results in grade twelve."

I barely passed grade eleven, and when I was in grade twelve, I didn't really know how to study for an A+ grade until a mentor of mine gave me some valuable advice that I hold dearly even today. She said, "If you are just consistent in grasping what was taught in class and do your homework regularly, you can score above ninety percent." Somehow, the driven kid in me who wanted to make her mother proud walked that advice. I was consistent and regular in class, and voilà! I topped my high school and shocked my family! It was one of the happiest moments of my life because it opened so many doors to prestigious schools. All it took was consistency and everyday practice. I was suddenly treated differently by everyone around me, from my peers to my school principal, and it was an amazing feeling.

When I was in my first year of university, I was introduced to my favourite philosopher, Fredrich Nietzsche. He conceptualized the idea of *Übermensch*, which means superman. I had to understand my own meaning of what it was from very long texts. What stood out to me was that for Nietzsche, a superman was someone who was no longer attached or lived their life by what others prescribed as goals or checkmarks to be successful. Instead, they'd set their own goals and were able to work toward achieving them. Years later, during late-night musings, the thought of *Übermensch* emerged in my heart. It is literally possible for all of us to be a superman or superwoman!

Find Comfort in Discomfort

"This is a ruthless world, and one must be ruthless to cope with it." —Charlie Chaplin

Growing up, no one taught me that self-control, self-monitoring, and self-discipline are the biggest challenges we face. It is so hard to set goals and whip oneself to achieve them. Most people I would talk to about their careers or goals had one thing in common: they all wanted to be billionaires so they could own luxurious things. I won't lie, so did I. We all grow up wanting to be the next big thing. Our idea of success is so engrained with owning wealth or being famous.

However, most times, when I met wealthy people, I found they were the most self-made miserable humans on earth! I'd ask why that was. They found the smallest reasons to harm their body or relationships and were very prone to alcoholism or pharmaceutical escapes. And heartbreak was the worst of them all to overcome. I saw many marriages of wealthy people in shambles or loveless because one person was carrying a scar so deep that they did not understand how to treat it.

In contrast, I saw people who were either middle class, poor, or underprivileged with far worse problems than the rich could even bear. Kids who grew up on the streets in poverty would get super happy when they would even get a bag of chips to eat, whereas kids who had an abundance of everything would still throw fits at their over-protective parents. People who made do with little income would find reasons to be grateful and happy. They'd even be more giving because they knew what it was like not to have, whereas the rich treated their house help like servants and people with less than them as a part of an inferior human race. I witnessed kids with the privilege of access to the best food in the world become stricken with health issues, and kids who survived on the bare minimum were the healthiest and fittest of them all!

After I had crossed twenty-five years and was still not a millionaire, I realized I had no other choice but to first be content with what I had. I was very much in control of myself and my emotions compared to my peers, who had rich parents to pay for their education, international trips, and designer attire. They were often battling depression and resisting hard work. Earning for myself and paying for the roof over my head made me self-reliant and unburdened. To be honest, lack of comforts or a money pillow can motivate us to work hard. When I bought my own second-hand car and lived in my own 400-square-foot basement apartment,

I knew that there is no one to blame for my inability to support my lifestyle and no one to rely on for it either. I started questioning whether whatever we do has any meaning or purpose.

A job of a shoemaker is equally important as the job of the shoe brand's CEO. Do not work hard based on what you think you deserve; work hard for the means of utilizing your life. Imagine if all the janitors hated their jobs or all the construction workers didn't care to finish projects on time. It will literally halt everything else that is important too. Do not undermine the power of hard work; it has ways of taking you to places that your wildest imagination takes you. Everything starts from ground zero and builds up little by little from there. Hard work and discipline are an education in themselves; they enlighten us about our next step and the step after that.

I often wondered why some people were always in need of likes on social media or material possessions to derive their self-worth. Why was it so hard for people who already had a lot of comforts to succeed in either their career or personal maturing? They'd found reasons to be bogged down by life, or created problems in their minds that trickled down to their health, and some just got distracted. People with an available infrastructure to succeed painted a sorry picture to the world, and it was difficult for them with all their made-up hardships to sharpen their abilities. They couldn't see or understand that every single human being is going through something at any given time. The answer was comfort and being comfortable. We face setbacks in life but being comfortable with the way something feels and mulling in that feeling will eventually become a habit that defines our present and future.

After graduation, everyone sets out to become financially successful and many start by working on an average-salaried job for years to pay their inescapable bills, which are necessary for survival. They may eventually reach higher positions in an organization and become comfortable, but they tend to let go of their bodies and mind. They live as consumers by buying small things to make them temporarily happy, which never bring lasting contentment. This makes them buy more and waste their money on insignificant crap, all while making the rich richer. Other people end up inheriting their parent's business because they always knew that was an option. Some people may not have a vision for themselves, and if they succumb to a comfortable materialistic life, they let go of their inner growth, hobbies, fitness, and spiritual goals.

At some point in our life, we ALL get comfortable with mediocrity and eventually become mediocre ourselves. We become comfortable with our narrow visions of life, not believing in prayers and magic, and not believing in hard work. We waste time and attention on things that are insignificant in the larger scheme of things. We become comfortable eating mindlessly and gaining weight, with our reactions to day-to-day situations, with waking up late or with indulging in utter nonsense. We focus on what is lacking or missing. We waste time on social media, consuming unnecessary content. We come comfortable blaming others, and become comfortable not reading or stimulating our minds. In the worst scenarios, we become comfortable drowning ourselves in drugs or alcohol. We become so comfortable with things that don't push us forward that they only make us live the same day and experiences over and over again. Eventually, it becomes our habit and, ultimately, our personality.

We forget to self-monitor, yet we easily criticize others for doing the same. Our growth stalls after a certain point, and we unwillingly accept the reality that we create. We forget all the dreams that we once had for ourselves. With the incessant thoughts that we fill our minds with, we leave no room for imagination.

Nurture Your Imagination

"One must still have chaos in oneself to be able to give birth to a dancing star." —Friedrich Nietzsche

As a child, we have so much space in our brains due to inexperience and innocence that it's easier to imagine and believe in all the impossibilities of the world. We happily believe in fairy tales, Santa, magic wands, and fantasy elements because our mind can imagine it so vividly that it all seems real. As we grow up to our twenties, thirties, forties and so on, all that diminishes because our mind starts riding on what we constantly fill it with.

It is harder to control the mind as we grow older because it is filled with so much crap from over the years that we have forgotten to discard. Meditation, or simply discarding the old, becomes harder to do because we are scared of sitting with ourselves and having all our thoughts come to the surface. It is so so so important that we sit in moments of silence each day, especially before beginning our day. We have so many opportunities to do it, and one of the best places can even be on a toilet! How will you stack more clothes in your closet if it's already filled with years and years of clothes? Having a bigger-sized closet is definitely one option, but having a bigger head isn't. When we keep adding new additions to our wardrobe, at times, an outfit we once loved and have only worn once gets lost in the pile.

All great cooking recipes were created by accident, like chocolate chip cookies! Similarly, all the experiments that we have lived through were the ingredients that led us to our present moment. Whether good or bad, everything and everyone played a role in defining who we are. The moment we accept that, a sense of ownership and gratitude kicks in. Instead of looking back with regret, look back with utmost acceptance, thankfulness, and appreciation. Everything was exactly how it was supposed to be to lead you to your true self. Wearing the same unwashed T-shirt every day makes us feel untidy and crusty, and wearing a washed, nice-smelling, clean T-shirt makes us feel refreshed and cozy. Washing and ironing our thoughts with some acceptance and gratitude can turn our minds around from a gritty state.

Meditation helps us become self-aware of what we lack and where we are strong. It helps us discover what does not serve us so we can discard it and discover how to enhance our life by getting to know ourselves better. Meditation allows our minds to grow and imagine possibilities. It allows us to appreciate our life with what is and what is not. It is an act of self-love and self-preservation.

People often find themselves lost with no direction or sense of control over their lives. When we introspect in moments of silence, we explore how we experienced something, why something did or did not work, and what kind of a setback we may be facing on a deeper level. The next steps of what to do to move forward happily will unfold before us.

We are our best teachers; there is a lesson in everything that has worked for us and everything that did not. Losing a loved one is the biggest reminder that human life is temporary, and we must do whatever it takes to live our best selves every single day. We have to learn from our mistakes to feel at peace. The more we draw out our takeaways from an event, the more we will mature and understand. However, we cannot find those lessons if we don't even have the mindset to seek them. Meditation, spending time with nature, and spending time with oneself is an act of self-love.

It's a discipline one needs to make a habit of, especially in this era when it is so easy to be distracted or manipulated.

Once we start loving our existence and only use our mind to focus on positivity, what we are capable of, whether it is in our career, personal life, or social life, answers will emerge.

Wake Up Early

"Well begun is half done." —Aristotle

The best time to spend some much-needed alone time is during early mornings between 4 and 6 a.m. In the holy texts of Sikhism, a religion that means "student of life," there is a verse that states, In the holy hours of the morning before the dawn, the rainbird (a pied cuckoo, *Clamator jacobinus* that looks like a small hawk) asks the sky, "Where is my love?" Then, listening to its cry, God summons the cloud to rain so it can quench the thirst of the bird. Whatever you are seeking comes to light during that time.

In astrology, Venus is the planet of beauty, love, and creativity, and it rises in the sky before the sun. Waking up during that time takes effort, a discipline that can unveil our own greatness within. Nature wakes in those hours, so why can't we?

To wake up that early, one must sleep early. Our human body does not need exactly eight hours of sleep;

it needs a good quality of sleep. When you sleep and wake up with nature, you tune yourself to the laws of nature. You will truly understand that when you own a dog, no matter what day it is, your dog will wake you up early morning for its business.

As we add hours to our day, we add hours to our life. Hours to work on ourselves and our goals, and slowly, we can add years to our life when we wake up at the holy and divine hours of dawn. The productivity, creativity, and physical strength that we receive as a gift from the divine between 3 and 6 a.m. is very special and truly a gift of our efforts. Our entire day is dedicated to eating, working, studying, running errands, and doing chores. It leaves little time for our soul, which is our battery. It is a discipline to sleep early and wake up early.

Waking up early already puts you ahead of people who are fast asleep until after sunrise. Use that time to meditate, work out, and drink lemony warm water so you can tackle the day the way you want it to be tackled. Beat the traffic, be the first in line to get your coffee, be the first person to respond to all the emails, and be the first person to finish first!

Listen to Your Teacher

"Self-control is the chief element in self-respect, and self-respect is the chief element in courage." —Thucydides

All the successful people we see whose craft we might think is undeserving of the credible stature they have earned are still better because they are self-made, and it took struggle and conviction In themselves to get them where they are. They might be negatively influencing a section of people or encouraging mediocrity, but the truth is that we cannot take away from their hard work because hard work always pays off. There will always be haters of unabashed women in the entertainment business, but it takes immense effort and courage to not be shy in front of the camera and just perform. Celebrities who pull in crowds irrespective of their art help provide a livelihood to so many people, like costume designers, choreographers, directors, writers, make-up artists, light directors, et cetera. Furthermore, their craft is used to run television channels, talk shows, and these days it even provides a career to so many Instagram and YouTube commentators. All that is possible because of team effort. We have to be the piece of the puzzle that is missing in a team and it is our job to make ourselves credible by firstly doing the best we can with what we have in our hands and not simply wishing to be rescued by some money-fairy. Success is not a stroke of luck or destiny; it's a result of your daily habits. Certain habits can lead us to a stronger conviction in our beliefs, ideas, and capabilities.

If you set a goal to be an artist, first work on your art. Learn, practice, perfect it, get critiqued, and be adaptable. Be consistent, forgive yourself for letting go of your resolutions, and remember to begin each day anew. We are humans who falter. Dust yourself off and get back in the race again. Do not let the comfort of babying yourself become a habit. Instead, push yourself and fight the inner demon that pulls you down.

A good meal is a result of good ingredients cooked in heat. No one can ignite the fire within you to be the best version of yourself. Discipline is the heat we need to make something of ourselves. That discipline results in hard work, sincere work, and good work. Use your precious energy for self-growth, and don't give in to things that do no good for you. Be mindful of where you spend your energy, avoid drama, avoid unnecessary aggravation, and do something that will release feel-good emotions. Creating certain consistent, life-enhancing habits is powerful. It gives you less time to waste on mindless internal chatter and gives you greater control over what you think, feel, and create for yourself. The results are instant.

Discipline is the foundation of self-love, and self-love leads to confidence. Confidence to tackle any situation that life throws at you. A confident person is comfortable with themselves, with others, and in every scenario, and that is such a sexy quality in a human being. Discipline is the catalyst to accelerating your walk toward a destination you desire. Everyday acts of self-love—like combing your hair to aid blood circulation or consistent yoga practice—are discipline.

Discipline isn't as scary and demanding of a concept as it sounds when it's done with the intention of love for oneself; discipline is nothing more than an act of self-love. If you want to change your environment, you have to change yourself first because it all begins from within. It is the vision corrector that we want to put on our eyes to see things clearly. Discipline is a routine, a consistency one cannot do without any day, and principles one beholds to define their life by. If we cannot come with little everyday positive habits that constitute our lives' discipline, then we are somewhere failing our lives. Discipline is the key to confidence in life; it makes you gain a stronger control of self. Discipline leaves little room for excuses that we make when we aren't feeling good about our present. Discipline is not only a physical attribute, but also a guideline for the thoughts we would like to promote within. Make self-love and self-improving habits a discipline to align yourself to a higher elevation of life.

Chapter Ten

Law of Attraction

"If you take care of the small things, the big things take care of themselves. You can gain more control over your life by paying closer attention to the little things."
—Emily Dickinson

I am sure we have all read several memes or quotes on the internet regarding the law of attraction: think positive to attract positive, karma, et cetera. And yet, no one seems to have the patience for the wise words. In fact, some people believe that a positive mindset means re-enforcing what they believe or are doing as an absolute. That very shallow approach will not result in attracting positive things in life. Instead, the opposite of our intentions usually manifests.

Dream Big

*"Yesterday is history. Tomorrow is a mystery. And today?
Today is a gift. That's why we call it the present."*
—Eleanor Roosevelt

I grew up in a middle-class family where both my parents worked hard. We lived in a two-bedroom house that was built in the 1950s. It was so old that the walls at one time started chipping, and we did not even have a proper door at the entrance. We shared one bathroom amongst five people, and there weren't dedicated living, dining, or study spaces. There was one room with a maroon carpet, where everyone slept together on the floor because it was the only room with an air conditioner and Indian summers are excruciatingly hot. We used to eat the simplest food and did not get spoiled with many toys. Our toy was our television, which used to witness massive fights over the remote control and sometimes even a power outage for a couple of days at a time.

When I was younger, we could never afford anything fancy or luxurious, and I always used to curse my parents for being cheap. I wasn't aware at the time that they were doing the best they could. Now that I look back, those were some of the best days of my life. They were the times when I was the closest to my parents. While being snug, we watched a rented movie every weekend with the whole family on our DVD player.

Watching a movie together with everyone on a tiny television was even better than watching it in a theatre.

Like I mentioned before, I used to love listening to my music player on the terrace while staring at the sky, especially during monsoon season. The breeze and the smell of the earth were so magical that they made me feel like there is something out there, something behind the stars gazing at us to know what we desire. With the sound of music plugged in my ears, I used to gaze away into space and visualize what I wanted, like a separate bedroom where I could have my privacy and keep a nice cellphone and camera in the drawers of my own side table. I used to think about owning nice outfits and branded sneakers like the ones in fashion magazines. I used to dream about my parents owning a nice house with neat interiors so I wouldn't be ashamed of inviting my friends over. I made my daydreaming a habit, a means of escape from the congestion of downstairs, by climbing onto my terrace every single evening.

I started to imagine going somewhere far away, where there would be no restrictions, and I could do and eat anything I wanted. I'd daydream about moving to live the American dream and study at a North American university. That dream seemed impossible because the cost of education alone was almost $25 000 a year. That was more than my parents' annual income at the time. But it didn't stop me from daydreaming about being a self-made girl who was living the life of a rock star.

A couple of years later, my parents' businesses started doing really well, and they ended up buying me the best cellphone. They even started renovations of our house. I eventually got my own bedroom with a purple bed, air conditioner, and two side tables (with drawers!). Our renovated house had new lamps, a computer on an office desk with an office chair, a new cupboard, a prayer room (yes, my mother's first priority), a dining room and a living room, but we still shared one bathroom. My parents got a brand-new car, and we even got a monthly allowance! They allowed me to eat all the junk and buy all the clothes that I had ever wanted to buy, but it didn't change my lack of freedom.

A couple of years after that, I ended up moving continents to study at a university in Ottawa, Canada. I could not believe all my daydream visions had come to life. Years later, while reminiscing, I realized that we have been blessed with a secret superpower of visualization that we can use to create anything we want for ourselves. I was able to visualize those things because I did not have those things in the first place. That void made me realize what I wanted to feel abundant. I knew that to experience freedom, I needed to move away from home.

By spending all that time with myself on the terrace visualizing, I recognized my likings and dislikes. It made me think about how I could live to be happy and have my freedom. I was never an A-grade student, but I started with dreaming so deeply that I couldn't even stop myself from working hard in my academics—I knew it would take me where I wanted to be.

As a child, I could visualize all those things for myself because my mind wasn't filled with the over-thinking that adulthood brings. I also did not have a better understanding of how to fulfill short-term, on-the-surface needs. I used my power of imagination on insignificant details rather than something more meaningful. That helped me realize our superpower within—all humans possess an ability to dream big. Since it's our dream, it can be whatever we like. The sky is the limit. This special ability is our magic wand, and sometimes even the angels are listening, but every dream requires us to tune ourselves to that frequency.

Live Within Your Means

> "We are not rich by what we possess but by what we can do without." —Immanuel Kant

In my previous chapter, I mentioned that most people dream of becoming a billionaire or at least filthy rich. They all want yachts, luxury cars, and mansions. There is nothing wrong with imagining how our lives would change if we possessed these things, but little empha-sis is placed on how it would make us feel. When we think about possessing tangible things, we forget to ask ourselves how we will bring them into our lives.

While at university, I looked up to many celebrities in media, entertainment, and philanthropy. I admired their conviction in themselves. I also wanted to become like them, rich and famous, but I wasted too much time on quick guilty pleasures, like gluing myself in front of a screen or partying. Sometimes just buying a nice (affordable) outfit to go out would give me a high, but I was wasting time and sidelining my education. It happens to most of us; we get so mesmerized by the sheer glamour of someone successful that we do not see the amount of conviction and work it took for them to reach there.

We all want instant results and for things to just fall in our lap without having a direction to work toward it. When I started working as a cashier at the food court in my university (while wearing a really ugly uniform and a hairnet), I became pals with my co-workers from various backgrounds and age groups. Though they were not financially well-off people, most of them were sweet, compassionate, kind, hardworking, dedicated, and sincere at their jobs. We'd serve entitled students who would make a mess without thinking of the workers who then slogged to clean it while always being under pressure from the management.

If everyone was rich, successful, and famous, who would do these jobs? Who would be the much-needed janitor, general help, cleaner, food-chopper, sandwich-maker, retail store salesperson, cashier, and, most important and angelic of them all, the pizza deliverer? If all of us collectively did not do our jobs sincerely, how would we contribute to the economy and essential services? How would we create a society that is less egoistic and more in harmony?

I started gaining respect for all the jobs that I thought were inferior or did not classify as elite. I feel grateful and blessed that I had to work at laborious jobs because it made me realize the importance of every single person on this planet. Every job plays a role in the larger scheme of things.

When I started working, I made $700-$800 a month, and I used that to pay my rent, bills, and keep some money aside for recreation and savings. A limited salary allowed me to live the best I could with what I had, and eventually, I found a job that paid me double that amount. That's when my expenses grew accordingly.

Follow Your Dreams

"I have always thought the actions of men the best interpreters of their thoughts." —John Locke

At my core, I always wanted to be a writer. I thought I could share my attitude of gratitude, but I did not know if it could be a career I could monetize and make a living off. To be honest, I wasn't even that sure of my craft, but I still wanted to write. I was stuck in a *rat race* of working 40 hours a week to pay my bills and I did that wholeheartedly because I knew it would help me save enough to take some time off for myself someday, which I will use to focus on my dreams.

In university, during my free time between classes, I was hanging out with my neighbour on her thirty-eighth birthday. She was cool—she sold weed and had a really cute dog. Her great taste in music, fashion, and movies brought us closer as friends. She came from a wealthy family and told me how she always thought she would do something big. She took time for granted, and before she knew it, she was thirty-eight. She said one of the most profound things that I tied under my belt. She said, "If you want to do something, do it now, or life will just go by and you will always live with regret."

That hit hard, but I still did not sit down to write. I kept dreaming because I had read a book about daydreaming and thought that if I daydream about a grand life, it will just fall into my lap. A few years went by with disappointment and frustration. After graduating, I worked at an entry-level position and slowly moved around different departments with a two-percent increase in my salary each move. It was good, and I was grateful. I got to meet all kinds of people and learn about corporate culture with all its vexing politics, but it never fulfilled me. Those feelings of frustration, unhappiness, lack-of, inferiority, unworthiness, and depression always dangled in me.

I would just sit and watch successful people on YouTube and wish I had what they had. The more I started listening to and about successful self-made people, I realized how much hard work they had to put in to get to where they were. There were many failures and embarrassments along the way, and they had to endure lots of discouragement—especially from people they knew—to reach the top.

Those people were working a hundred times harder than I was. They worked on their fitness and their minds to stay in high spirits and to have self-belief. They worked not just on their craft with discipline, but they forced themselves to detach from things that brought their spirits down. When I was working, deep inside knew I could do better. I wanted to feel like I mattered and not be just another disposable employee who used up all her salary to pay bills.

Eventually, it hit me that life wouldn't become better when I have lots of money. It's just getting wasted by not being the best version of myself right here and right now. I had no other choice than to make the best of what I had at the time. I made time to go to the gym, focused on eating to fuel the body, and found happiness in little things that were going for me. But when I was at work, being rich or beautiful also did not matter. All that I cared about was being productive, contributing to the team, and becoming a highly skilled person.

We often forget that it's not the tangible stuff that we crave. We crave respect from others and self-respect. We wish to realize our purpose and do things that make us want to jump out of our bed every morning. Most importantly, we want to do things that make us feel independent and in control of our happiness.

We all want to feel special in our lives, and the only person who can make us feel that is ourselves. No material object or experience can ever make us feel that. Yes, certain experiences can cause a new dawn within, but it's how we use our mind and body that ultimately determines the journey we will embark on.

Instead of focusing on shallow, dead-end goals that do not make us feel at peace, we should focus on our permanent attributes, graceful behaviours, elegant personalities, higher visions, healthy bodies, and a positive mindset. We must aim to be the best version of ourselves at all times. When we are at our best at all times, that high that we will feel, whether we are financially successful or partnered up with someone we love, is unmatched and is truly aligned with our inner self.

I learned that to get promoted in a corporate environment, we must already be doing the duties and job of that desired position to be considered a desirable candidate. Similarly, when we desire a promotion of our status in life, we should already be working toward it. We should have an elevated mindset and be ready when the opportunity knocks, not start working after we have the promotion. That will disappoint our bosses and lead to us eventually getting fired or demoted. Life and the universe work very similarly. We have to be deserving of what we desire. We just can't desire without deserving.

There is no heavy rainfall in the desert; it's just not possible given the climatic conditions. Our status in life cannot improve if our actions and mindset are the opposite of what we desire. Young people who attained fame and wealth in their teens are most prone to mental health issues because they suddenly jumped from zero to a hundred on a jam-packed highway. We can't jump from the ground floor to the eleventh floor in one go. We must take the stairs or an elevator and go through each floor to get to the top.

Every day, every lesson, every person who comes and goes, every experience, every inexperience, every lack thereof, every moment, and every setback is our climbing ladder to the top. It's happening because we needed it to become who we are in this very moment. We have to be accepting and grateful for what is right here and right now. This is not the destination. It's only a step in our journey.

At times, I feel so grateful to God for not giving me what I desired because years later, I realized it could have been the worst thing for me. I wasted so much time wanting a thing or a person in my life that I later realized were insignificant and not what I needed. Time is our biggest teacher if only we are willing to learn. Always ask God to give you what you deserve because you deserve much more than you desire.

As a child, we always cry to our parents for sugary treats, not knowing that sugar is bad for us. We reject fruits and vegetables even though they help us stay healthy and happy because we are not aware or do not have the cognitive ability to understand. Time heals and teaches us all, and sometimes, taking a deep breath to make sense of why something is, is the best thing you can do for yourself.

When we don't constantly keep asking or wanting things from the universe or God, we vibrate at a frequency of contentment and acceptance. When we are fully immersed and utilizing the things we have in the present moment, we start being grateful. We start respecting and cherishing what we have or don't have.

Look back at the best days of your life. Some you might remember, and some you might not. Even the best days of our lives don't have any power over our present moment. This should make us realize that like bad days pass, good days also fade, and we must live in full awareness of what we have. Sometimes the bad days that have passed with time don't even seem that bad at all because they prepared us for what is to come. The only regret is we often carry a lack of judgment of the situation or poor performance with us as a burden.

Luck is a result of our wholesome hard work and opportunities. After working for several years at a job, I was eventually let go and it broke my heart, but that setback helped me to commence my new journey as a writer. All the experiences that I had gained from previous years could only come from experiencing what I needed to at the time in order to type my thoughts onto a screen. Looking back, it was all the adversities that brought me closer to my big dream of being a writer.

Nothing is difficult to achieve. One must just be consistent, willing, and ready to use one's limbs to put the work in. Daydreams will not materialize unless you work on yourself and where you want to get to. A doctor has to study for years with dedication before they can run their own clinic, and land must be dug and primed first before constructing a building on it. We do not get anything in life unless we work for it.

Yes, we get opportunities, and yes, we get all the pre-requisites to set up shop. But unless you run the show, nothing will come out of it. I received the bare minimum of what I had daydreamed from the universe, but that was not what I thought would bring me purpose. Eventually, a lack of purpose attracts a lack of work. The best reward is our intentions, a realization of life's purpose, and a path to work hard in itself.

How can you dream of becoming a successful businessman when you never wish to know within yourself what it is that you can trade or provide to society. Not everyone is born knowing what they want to do, but we always have an internal voice guiding us toward what we should do. We muddy it with procrastination and negative self-beliefs, or we distract ourselves by indulging in instant highs.

Time just passes, our dreams become stale, and we cry in vain. The ideas that spark within us are what we must work on. We must visualize the success of our idea instead of letting negative self-talk take over. As long as we intend to do things that do not harm, cheat, or hurt anyone and only uplifts us and those around us, even the universe helps us succeed.

When we are only daydreaming, wanting things but walking the opposite way, then it will be a long time before we will come back home.

We will unknowingly search for reasons to make excuses, and we will cause drama or have expectations from others because we don't feel fulfilled ourselves. We will always long for the company of others because our own company makes us feel gloomy. We will always take the things we have and that others dream of for granted. What is the use of earning and acquiring those things if they can't even make you feel joyful?

If you want to play a Top 40 radio station in your car, but the radio is tuned to a news station, how do you expect your radio to understand what you want to hear? The radio's frequency is a direct comparison to our life. The satellite uses radio waves to channel the desired frequencies from point A to point B, and sometimes we drive through a tunnel with low network coverage that causes a disruption, but that too passes. We are in constant communication with every wave and every energy that we emit, and we are actively transmitting signals from ourselves to attract what we have tuned ourselves to. If we are not even aware of this fact, we are only causing confusion and disruptions to ourselves.

Trust the Cosmos

"He who is not contented with what he has, would not be contented with what he would like to have." —*Socrates*

We don't attract what we think we should attract; we attract who we are. We are the words we speak, the thoughts we think, the work we do, and the food we eat. We exist based on the way we perceive life and ourselves, how we treat others, the dedication we hold, the people we surround ourselves with, the opportunities we seize, and the attitudes we behold.

Our main challenge in life is to first and foremost be the best version of ourselves irrespective of circumstance. I was once sitting on my balcony in Ottawa and listening to a very famous Canadian hip hop artist called Drake. One of the lines in his song that I was extremely enchanted by mentioned that all the pretty girls live off of Markham Road in east side of Toronto. Being clueless about which place he was talking about at the time. A few years later, I was living off Markham Road in the east end, which is a suburb, neighbouring Toronto. We are unintentionally attracted to some things in our lives that are truly meant for us, and what we engrain in our feelings the most becomes our reality.

If you choose the path of greatness in every inch of your body and every facet of yourself, greatness will chase you. How can you undertake big efforts when the smallest are the hardest to be consistent with? Everything big begins with something small. Once the focus is on the now, the focus on what is to come is lessened, which reduces anxiety of the unknown.

God helps those who help themselves; it all begins from within you. Once the high of living in happy spirits and creating what you desire kicks in, a sense of detachment from the "what if" embodies itself. It becomes amazing to be happy with what you have and what is the best you can do in the current situation. Those little victories stay in our hearts forever. If we are happy, content, enjoying our life, grateful, and optimistic, then life will only give us reasons to be happier, content, grateful, and to see the positivity in and around us.

The law of attraction is real; we must shift our focus from witnessing the lack of things to recognizing the abundance in our lives. Gratitude isn't just being thankful. Rather, real gratitude is when we fully utilize and give the highest regard to the things we have, from our health to our ability to dream. If we choose to be abundant and be detached from things that pin us down, then we are only attracting things that will make us feel more abundant.

Chapter Eleven

God

"True wisdom comes to each of us when we realize how little we understand about life, ourselves, and the world around us." —Socrates

Who really is God? Ironically, it's the least and the most answered question of human existence. Many prayers are answered; many are not.

Religions have instilled in us the ideas of hell and heaven and that there's some supreme being sitting out there in space. Some set forth principles for how to be a good human by abiding by the rules of that religion. Different religions believe in no drinking, no sex before marriage, no cutting of hair, wearing a specific attire, eating specific foods, reciting prayers in a specific direction, and following certain traditions. In some religions, disciples worship angels, saints, deities, solar eclipses, or crystals. However, all religions claim to have found the answer or path to God. I am a Sikh, and in my religion, we feel divinity by singing the glorious praises. Music is how we worship the dear Lord within and around us and something about music . . . it has the power to connect us all.

Compared to previous centuries, today's world is different, and in most parts of the world, people are loosening up and becoming more accepting of each other's religious beliefs. However, there are many pockets in the world where there is concentration of only one religion or culture, which makes it difficult for younger generations to discover their own idea of God. In those places, everything is already predetermined. It's predetermined what people should believe in and which faith offers the best and quickest way to the dear Lord above.

Extremists believe that God loves a specific religion more than the others. This division of people is deeply rooted, and it goes back for centuries. In the end, the biggest beneficiary has been the religious leaders. Being religious these days is sometimes seen as being uncool because of this association.

The Nature of Worship

Our understanding of greatly evolved humans who reflected the closest description of divine, who mastered the skill of letting go, rose above greed, or were chari-table, has been jumbled up to think of them as gods. However, they are merely guardians of love on earth.

Before the internet or digital devices with social media platforms were a thing, there used to be a mys-tical aura around movie stars, politicians, entertain-ers, and performers, so much so that people used to worship them like gods. There was so much mystery around these media stars because we only saw them on the big screens. At times, we even thought that they were the character they portrayed.

At the time, the limited availability of different tech-nological mediums made it difficult for many people to become successful in the media. This meant that only a handful of actors would rule the theatres and other fame-stages. Many people blindly worshipped famous entertainers and rich businessmen, yet they were secretly drug abusers or sell-outs who just wanted to accumulate wealth by advertising anything, from fairness creams to fizzy, sugar-filled drinks.

Recently, with the rise of video and image-sharing platforms, many talented people have surfaced. Everyone's willing to do just about anything to get attention or followers, like posting what they eat or what they wear. People have made careers out of any-thing and everything. The competition is so vile that someone is being exposed every second day or people just start behaving like utter lunatics to get traction.

More than ever, we can clearly see who these people are; they are people just like us with a different job and the only difference is that they are more unapologetic and okay with putting themselves out there. Stories that have passed down for generations about religious figures often have no solid proof of who they really were as people. What these idols once said or preached has been misinterpreted with each interpretation.

How can God exist in only one human, and why should they declare that a specific section of humans is the best and all that it cares about? If that was truly the case, why did God suddenly stop re-emerging in the form of a human after the advancement of communication and technology? Why is God not on Facebook?!

There have been and will always be many wise men and women who have discovered, researched, and practised a way of being that is more freeing and less burdensome. In this existence, it's important to be ethical, compassionate, just, and rational. Such people uplift others' spirits and set examples of how to be happy and content, how to believe in magic and hope, how to look within and have self-belief, and how to love thyself. This is beautiful. Like our bodies, our minds also need a trainer to help us navigate through life.

Some of the greatest advice passed down by religious gurus has been to live based on a geographical condition, eat certain foods, stay natural with what you were born with, love your family, be charitable, believe, and have faith. These amazing humans have discovered the art of living, which means being in tune with nature. Some wake up early to recite powerful words that induce self-belief and a sense of power (also called prayer). Others discovered that fasting helps detox our body, which is much needed in today's world of synthesized foods. Others encourage marriage as a way to solidify a companionship with someone we can have an everlasting bond with, and not just to give yourself to anyone to fill a void. All this advice has come from humans; no one could fly or disappear in the sky, no one could change their size or breathe fire. They were humans, just like we are.

Discover Your Form of Godliness

From my teens to my early twenties, I had moved around twelve times and lived in three different cities by myself. This prevented me from having a boyfriend or maintaining any reliable, stable, or lifelong friendships. I just met temporary people, most of whom did not even qualify as friends; they were more like acquaintances. I had no girlfriends with whom I could really be honest, and no family close by, so I spent every Christmas and birthday alone or at an acquaintance's family gathering as an outsider. The charm of being with different people started to fade, and after a point, I started craving something solid.

At the time, I felt insignificant to the people I hung out with. I felt that they'd hang out with me only if they had nothing better to do. I was anxiety-stricken, phobic of everything, paranoid, and would look for temporary escapes to drown my loneliness. For about ten years, I slept with the lights at night on because I was scared of burglars and ghosts. Any tiny sound would wake me, so the only thing that helped me sleep securely was religious music. I thought it would ward off evil spirits. During the day, I spent my time working six to seven days a week to tire my body and mind to sleep. The more effort I put in to keep friends interested, the more cynical and bitter I grew about the world.

I turned to prayers and religious music, and I started to really hold onto the powerful words written by our ancestors, such as "no one can give or take from you other than God" or "you are a part of God, recognize yourself and act accordingly." I did not truly know what it meant, but somehow it seemed to soothe my soul. Sometimes, it'd even make me break into tears.

In my utmost state of solitude, no friend, no guy, no family came to rescue me from the darkness that grew inside me. One night, after a few glasses of wine, I looked at myself in the mirror. I cried horrifically, called out to God, and I asked why he had forgotten about me. Why was I so lonely, and why wasn't he coming to rescue me? Or did he even exist?

I woke up the next day as usual. I packed my lunch, made my smoothie, and got ready for work. But something weird happened that day. When I was returning from work, I unintentionally drove right in front of the Sikh temple called Gurdwara. I went inside the temple, bowed my head in front of our holy book, then went back home and somehow, I wasn't not feeling as bitter and jaded as I had the day before.

With each day after that, I found myself listening to religious music more and more. It was a push to keep myself occupied in self-indulgent activities and at peace when I slept alone. I slowly started becoming perfectly comfortable being by myself. I'd even use my alone time in productive ways, like reading books that I had bought from thrift stores or appearing as a background cast member for TV shows and movies. Some people, like my landlord or property manager at work, even started helping me with anything that I needed, like a latch on my door or hanging my TV on the wall. I started feeling like I was cared for and had people to help me with little things. I had none of that before.

With time, holy classical music that wasn't about a particular God started to uplift my spirits and helped me work on myself. Even though I have never met God in some obvious form, I started feeling the love in my heart and mind. I started feeling safe and secure, and most importantly, I started feeling like it will all be okay. That is when I first realized God in my life in the form of love.

That magical feeling of love is so powerful that even my words cannot describe the beauty of it. It's not something you can read or touch; it is something to feel. Unless you find a way to bring God into your own life, you will never be able to feel the power of this magic. It requires patience, just as everything that grows requires patience. But sometimes, if you are lucky, flying in love can happen overnight.

The Power of Prayers

Prayers are beautiful. They are beautiful affirmations that uplift our spirit. The art and creativity involved have the power to change our entire state of mind. Learning about ancient knowledge and its ensuing wisdom creates harmony amongst people and families by adhering to a certain tradition. Creating a family through marriage by making an eternal promise and participating in communal activities like serving the needy have the power to unite and bring families and people closer together. To evolve collectively and belong to a sect of people with a similar culture and language are wonderful attributes that humans and religions have created. However, to impose them as obligations or to confine goodness only in man-made buildings is highly limiting and hypocritical.

It's like we have decided that God is some kind of a ruler who we must obey, or we will get punished. If God is the ultimate punisher, why did religious leaders make laws and the consequences of breaking those laws? I know many religiously religious people who have many faces. Some are so judgmental they cannot even love their own children without expectations. These people are unaware of what they are reciting in their prayers. The discipline of praying and wearing specific attire has become the primary focus rather than walking the talk. We often find these people gaining popularity in the media.

In Hinduism, there is mighty *Lord Ganesh* (which we in North America call the Elephant God). He is basically a mix of an elephant and a human in a miraculous form of life. No one has a real photograph of the Lord, but there are artistic interpretations. An artist with his own vision and creativity drew Lord Ganesh's image, and several people have portraits of him in their homes. In flamboyant art galleries, people try to make sense of what the artist has created and sometimes, they need alcohol to decipher the haywire ruckus of colours. Lord Ganesh is an embodiment of human and animal combined. The instinct of animals combined with the intelligence of a human is a reflection of divinity within us. When applied in balance, both can lead us to a wholesome life.

Religious texts worldwide carve beautiful psychological lessons and preach pragmatic approaches to life. It's a way that helps us realize the best of ourselves. Reading is a powerful means to stimulate our minds. Many religious texts, when read over and over again, have a chance of aligning our personality with their wise words. They guide us to an optimal way of living, and when we make something a habit, it becomes our personality. When we truly live based on who we are, then we only attract that.

People have altered many things to satisfy their palettes. We have the cognitive capability to make judgments and decide what we do, but we often get corrupted when we interact with living beings less intelligent or weaker than us. We sometimes even make them our food. If God, who is running the entire universe, were to act the way we did, then none of us would be alive.

We know of its supreme existence, so why don't we all cater to him instead of the big conglomerates in our world? No one would have the power to change society as many businesses do in our world. People often ask this question, "If God exists, then why do bad things happen to good people?" But the question is never, "Why do good things also happen to good people?" It's not God doing bad things unto people; it's our fellow humans committing ill toward each other for their greed and beliefs.

It's in our nature to build dominance over what we can control. We often ignore those who need us the most, including some family members who might be behind or struggling in their lives. Kids bully the weaker and shy kids more because they get a sense of power over the others. They lack the feeling of being needed or wanted unless they exert dominance with physical power or money. For a while, it will go on. But it's science—we reap what we sow. When humans attain riches and power, they tend to be corrupt or dismissive of the less powerful.

It's okay for God to tolerate our vices and to forgive us when we ask for forgiveness. However, we cannot tolerate anything that is not serving us, and we carry grudges until we die! We denote God with the qualities we are searching for in others, but not ourselves. God is as good as the languages we understand. If we can't understand another's language, we can never form a deep bond with them. We talk to God in our hearts because we have the skill of language to make ourselves understood. Conversations and understanding are the foundations of any bond and they have a power to get us through a stormy day.

Divine Creativity

For some people, God is as good as someone who grants them all their wishes. Who created life, planets, gravity, laws of nature, time, space, and the universe? We don't know, but all we know is that something was created in the beginning. It's been discovered that out of nowhere, there could have been an existence of energy or atoms, which blasted and spread across nothing, creating our very universe. This theory is known as the Big Bang theory, and scientists believe that if this was just nature doing its thing, then it's bound to happen again and again. However, the pertinent question that still remains is that there must be something around this energy or atom that "banged," and the scientists are trying to research those answers by searching inside the black holes of space. We still don't have a clear answer as to how or why the universe was created, but we do know that our world is a creation.

Everyone was created from that same source of energy. Animals don't have religious gods; we humans do because we are in the quest for enlightenment. Unlike humans, animals don't have a language that is understood universally, and they lack the cognitive (and sometimes physical) capacity to look up to the light.

We humans have also been doing our part by either creating babies or inventing hunting weapons. This is something we have in common with our initial creator, God, whether we create cooking recipes, languages, modes of transportation, clothes, or thoughts that become the actions of how we conduct ourselves. Regardless, we are all creating each day. When our spirits are low, we look to create something to make us feel good and alive. When we are in an energetic mood, we create adventurous experiences. Creativity tends to make us feel a sense of achievement and alive. It makes us feel like we serve some purpose.

God is Love

> "I searched for God and found only myself.
> I searched for myself and found only God." —Rumi

We think of God as someone who loves us unconditionally and will take care of us. We have the ability to love, which is another thing we have in common with God and animals. Love is not tangible or seen, but when our families or strangers love us, we feel so good. That good feeling leads us to so many positive experiences. It allows us to enjoy ourselves to the fullest.

A person could be reciting the same prayer a thousand times a day that states, "everything is created by God," yet be one to criticize and judge others or may consider themself superior or special. We must let our prayers create the feeling of acceptance and nourish the faith that everything is working in its desired order and nature. If we don't surrender our minds and temporary emotions to remember the greatness within, how can we unite with and understand our primary creator?

Love and creativity are the truest forms of God known and unknown to man. We cannot see them, but the feeling that lingers inside our minds and hearts after feeling the power of it is magical. Can we expect our dog or cat to suit up and sit in on board meetings or make grand speeches as a nation's leader? We cannot because pets are not physically capable of walking on two feet, and they do not possess the capability to speak like humans. Nature has created them to be four-legged creatures that know how to love, eat, poop, and sleep. Humans can connect with animals on the emotion of love and positive re-enforcement.

We might never find an answer to a question called God and we might not have been created intelligent enough to know God in the first place. We might not be able to handle the truth or be equipped to deal with the supreme knowledge. But what can unify us with

God is our need for love and the ability to create. Love for oneself first, then sharing the magic with others.

We spend too much time wanting to know God and little emphasis on the power we share. When we love, It makes us feel good, hopeful, and alive. It prevents us from being stuck in our mental chains. It allows us to expand our minds and imagine all the possibilities that will make us feel good. Loving the food we eat, the nature around us, the people we interact with, and the things we have (and don't have) strengthens our relationship with God. When we love, we create more of it.

We take our long lists of wants to God, but if we do not love it for its greatness unconditionally, then we ought to be disappointed. God gave us the power to create life by creating us. It gave us the power to love everything and stay in high spirits. We all have the power within; some of us just require more practise and effort than others, but the power still exists.

Love concocts a magical feeling within us. When our prayers are answered, how does it make us feel? It makes us feel heard and important, and it makes us feel powerful. An infant cannot comprehend what it is like to be an adult, and an adult cannot understand the maturity old age brings. Without loving all that is and all that is not, one cannot appreciate the magic that is created within. God himself shares the language of love and corresponds with you through that love to provide the answers one seeks.

Everyone's God is different, and everyone's God is a reflection of themselves. If you are expecting a lottery to be rich, then you will always believe in luck. If you love the body you have, the limbs you use, the food you eat, and the family you have, you can celebrate your happy days with all these things. Little things will become a means to count your blessings, and you will always feel like a lucky winner.

We all have our bad days, but the ability to create love within yourself in those times provides the ability to overcome anything. You can overcome a negative emotion by simply focusing on your ability to breathe—the essential function that is always supporting your life—then you have unlocked the secret of your power within that God has blessed you with.

You can talk to God by talking to yourself with love. All the answers and guidance will emerge from within you. It will guide you toward the best way to conduct yourself in any given situation. Our body is so intelligent that it automatically produces antibodies to fight a cut or an infection. We don't have to ask our body to create an immunity toward many diseases. When we fracture our bones, the bone, with time, heals itself. Our mind is so intelligent that it will find ways to cope with any setback if we fill it with faith and love.

We take the power of our body to fight for itself for granted. We don't sit and delve into the magic it beholds. When we make love our second nature, we give our mind the intelligence to guide us in any situation. Faith is not a daily reminder; faith should be our primary nature. Whatever is happening or is going to happen, it will all be okay.

God has given us a body that supports our life and an environment that can feed us and quench our thirst. God has given us the power to create what we want and the ability to give love to feel ecstatic. He loves us unconditionally, so must we love our life unconditionally.

Love + Creativity = Godliness

We are not meant to understand God. We are meant to share and connect with what we have in common; i.e., love and creativity. Our beliefs constitute our reality, and we must not feel victimized and make excuses. We must take charge and responsibility for what we want to feel at all times.

The universe has millions of galaxies, planets, comets, and many other problems to look after, so God gave us the ability to look after ourselves. For example: if you had a child, you wouldn't seek praise from them for your parenting efforts. Instead, seeing your child live happily and mindfully will make you feel content. When children are supportive of the struggles of their parents and use the wisdom and resources that their parents provide to their advantage, it makes the parents feel proud and secure. Similarly, you are God's creation, God's child. Use the wisdom it gave you, and don't cry for more shiny toys. Make God proud of you and love it back. Be content with what it gave you and what it did not.

God made us our own God. That's the greatest gift it could serenade us with, so now it is up to us what we do with our life. When our vision is weak, we wear corrective lenses or get eye surgery. If our power within us is weak, we must correct it with love. The greatest gift you can ask from God is to give you its love and wisdom within your heart. The rest of you is powerful enough to work hard, focus, and HOPE for the best.

If we cannot hope, then why do anything at all? We hope for our favourite sports team to win, or for us to pass an exam. Hope is another magical feeling that results from love and the belief to create the desired outcome you want.

Mankind's evolution is a result of intelligence and learning how to adapt to an environment. Rocks, plants, insects, animals, and humans were shaped by the environment they endured. If a species could not adapt and survive, it was eventually shredded by nature. We should be ever ready to learn, adapt, and evolve. We are not born with all the lessons; we learn as we go. If we know it all, then what is the point of living and discovering where and how we end up?

However one would like to decipher it, this is for sure: there is a God, energy, or someone supreme out there. It's not within our human intelligence to know what that entity is and where it resides. The common denominator between God and us is pure love toward everything inside and outside of us and the power to create. We have the power to create and to love. We can create something unique to us which might be of no significance to others. We can love someone or something creatively, differently than others. When you practice love and creativity, that is where you realize true devotion and worship.

Chapter Twelve

Hard Work and Success

"Whether you think you can, or you think you can't—you're right." —Henry Ford

Some people are born extremely privileged financially. Their parents are wealthy, and they don't have the same relationship to money as other kids in middle- or lower-class families. The upper-class ones may have grown up in a nicer house with a chandelier, drive nicer cars, and received a better education and all those privileges that are just a dream for others.

When they grow up well-off, they don't need to struggle for the basic necessities of life. The sword of paying bills isn't dangling over their heads, so they may seek enrichment in other areas of life. Eventually, it becomes second nature to be around nice things, so the glamour of materialism vanishes. Their minds wander to look for something to fill their time and fulfill their life. There is a possibility that the mind gets comfortable when needs are easily met that it does not thirst to expand itself beyond those comforts. Without that powerful feeling, the mind remains unstimulated, and an existential issue takes over.

What is Wealth?

Imagine winning a lottery worth a lot of money. What would you do? You would quit your job, buy a nice car, a nice house that you will spend time decorating, throw all the best parties, buy your family members gifts, travel, and hire a cleaner. All that is great, so now what do you wake up for after all your primary wants have been fulfilled? What comes after all the parties? Eventually, all the monetary pleasures will fade, and a sense of wanting to do something to be self-respected will creep in. Laying around to laze and relax all day isn't as fulfilling as one would think; it tires the body, messes up the spine, makes one simply dumb, and makes the days go by quicker.

Our idea of success is often associated with the idea of attaining wealth. I have come across wealthy people who have not worked hard (or at all) for their money, while some of the hardest-working people get paid close to minimum wages. Meanwhile, some countries don't even have minimum wage as a concept. Some people are rich by virtue of the geographical territory they were born in, and some are poor and marginalized due to their family's history of being the lowest in the economic chain.

Wealth is a very complex topic. It is crucial to living, it derives our self-worth, and it is instrumental in keeping a social life and buying experiences to feel a high. Everyone wants to be rich at their deep inner core, and who can blame us? Money provides a sense of security. It feeds us and makes us feel untouchable. We put so much emphasis on wanting money that products are not sold on the basis of need. Products are now innovated to create desire in the market and urge people to own things to feel empowered.

Even with all our stuff, true satisfaction is felt only after a nice meal and a good night's sleep. Good sleep and a good meal (if you are lucky) are the utmost basic things that very honestly bring calmness to one's day. However, we have found ways to reduce our positive experiences around meals and sleep. We stare at screens instead of talking to our families while eating or chewing food properly and due to that, we have increasingly slower digestion. When we push our bedtime and stare at a screen until we pass out, we enter a disturbed sleep.

Eat, Sleep, Work Hard

Nutrition and sleep are two aspects that one should take care of and feel grateful for. For some of us, both are second nature. If we don't recognize their existence, it can cause us to sabotage ourselves and ruin our basic engineering of peace and calm.

Our idea of peace is often aligned with owning wealth versus eating and sleeping. Wealth brings us security, but never peace or calm because it is not created by nature; it's created by man. It is not a natural occurrence; it is similar to drinking alcohol. Alcohol makes us feel lightheaded and hearted. It makes us daring or easy-going and, in some cases, extra social. But it wears off. We then tend to drink more of it to keep that feeling alive, but it only sabotages our health in return. It does feel great when we are immersed in it, but not so great after it leaves the body. Also, as one matures into drinking, one needs more to feel the same effects. So why do we consume it? Because it makes us high.

Wealth is the same. It allows us to enjoy social gatherings, we feel great when we have it and uneasy when we don't, and the more we have of it, the more we want to meet our growing wants. We think we own it, but eventually, its allure ultimately owns us. Hard work is truly a wealth and never goes unnoticed by the laws of nature. It always has a way of paying off!

In economics, the theory of utility states that our satisfaction from consuming a product declines from the first time it's utilized to the second, third, and so on. For example, if you love ice cream and have a fridge full of it. The first ice cream you consume will bring you the most satisfaction. The second ice cream you eat will diminish your sugary cravings, and the third ice cream may make you want to stop. You could feel less satisfied than if you had stopped after the first one.

When we don't have something, the allure of it is so much more in our eyes and minds. Once we own it, the allure fades, and we look for the next shiny toy. The more wealth we have, the more extreme our wants will be, which puts us on the path of never being satisfied. This is what happens to many people who attain instant success; they get so immersed in the glamour of it that their attention on what they want to do takes a backseat. It's always there, but it fades because our appetite gets distributed amongst too many things.

Our idea of prosperity is tied to owning wealth because it fulfills our primary short-term wants. It does not make us feel fulfilled or produce a sense of peace in our hearts. The entanglement of feeling satisfied, full, and nourished has confused many of us and our idea of success. We don't need a lot of wealth to be content or to lead a good life. We are still going to eat the same food, drive a car that takes us from point A to B, and live in a decent house or apartment. We will still be able to travel, even if it's in economy class. We'll always have the same parents and siblings and will still want to be loved. A five-figure income can do the same job as a six-figure income.

To aim for a livelihood that can give us a comfortable life is fair and important. Everyone with a basic education can attain that, depending on the country one is born in. But mindlessness arises when the idea of a comfortable living is confused with the idea of owning a lot of wealth. As long as people work to earn food and keep a roof over their heads, it is good enough. The satisfaction from a meal and a good night's sleep is the same across all humans.

For kids with wealthy parents, their compulsion to work hard may not be as strong as the idea of becoming more successful than their parents. Of course, this is not always the case, but it does happen. When we don't work to create the emotion that we want to feel, we start to get controlled by the emotions that are just freely flowing within us. When we don't focus on ourselves first, we create emotions that others want us to feel.

We are energetic beings, and we pick up on the energies around us. Our mind scatters so much that it creates a feeling of depression, which reduces our mind's ability to create its own happiness. This can happen when we use our intelligence on irrelevant things rather than creative and productive things. Everyone gets scatter-brained, distracted, and distributed, but we must focus back on what truly satisfies to bounce back to a sense of peace.

If we conceptualize and prioritize what brings us peace and what doesn't, we stop deriving our self-worth based on how much money we have. Money is not the goal. The goal is to sleep well and nourish the body, and money is only a means to enable that. We must engage our minds every day to work hard so we can feel tired and hungry, which allows us to sleep peacefully, enjoy our meals to the fullest, and create a sense of purpose in our lives.

Find Joy in Work

Every job or business that allows us to keep ourselves busy is the best circumstance we can find ourselves in. If we didn't have any obligations, we would waste our days moping around in bed or being a couch potato. Having something to do every day, and even better, doing something that you love, is beneficial. Eating right is hard work, working out is hard work, studying is hard work, working at a job for ten hours and then making a meal for the family is hard work, and taking time out for self-improvement is hard work!

Eventually, the results of hard work become irrelevant. The high of putting in the work is rewarding enough because it occupies our life and our brain, so we don't end up with time or energy to go on a downward slope. It makes us feel purposeful and gives us something to look forward to. It helps us organize our time, priorities, and our goals. "How to deal with a breakup" advice from magazines or blogs is usually to focus on yourself and do things that will make you happy. All of us respect ourselves more when we occupy our lives with something productive.

Everything special requires work. Plastic surgery can make your skin tighter, but the right diet and health regime can give you new skin! We do not put enough emphasis on the power of daily hard work. Occupying our life with goals instead of sitting on our bums with a lot of money in the bank becomes our heart's desire. The more we practice, the more it becomes a part of us. The more we slouch our backs, the curvier our spine gets with age. We must tune the frequency of our ethos to chase our ability to work hard. It will gradually pay off and make us grow, be independent thinkers, and feel a sense of hold over our lives.

Everyone works hard to take care of their families by paying the bills and taxes. Fulfilling those responsibilities is so stressful and demanding that taking care of ourselves by preparing a healthy meal or participating in extracurricular activity becomes secondary. We always need to work harder than we already do, whether in our professional or personal lives, to move ahead. Consistency and dedication to put in work slowly result in success.

It does not come overnight; it needs work and determination. The sun, moon, and earth are just doing their thing, each day, every day, tirelessly, naturally, and punctually. They are moving forward in time each day, based on their programming. We must make ourselves do the work consistently to keep us moving forward and bring order to our lives.

If we are chasing success, we must first live every day to be productive and successfully put in the hard work. Our thoughts instantly make excuses and build a procrastination scheme, but we must practice fighting our desires to be comfortable. Hard work is hard work in itself. Unless you are born rich, you have to be on top of your game to become rich and enjoy riches. Every single day one must learn to do the needful and fruitful.

Without discipline, consistency, and hard work, there is no success or fulfillment. Hard work in itself holds so much power psychologically, emotionally, mentally, and tangibly that the result of it becomes secondary. We undermine the power of hard work and hold ourselves back from doing it because it takes a lot of power and control over the mind to do it. Working hard is a blessing in itself; it is a privilege. It gives life a purpose and a road to be disciplined. If hard work were everyone's cup of tea, then everyone would be employed and successful in life.

The more we embrace it, the more success it will result in. Everything long-lasting and fulfilling requires hard work—hard work on oneself and hard work to pay bills. Nothing comes easy, but everything can go easy. Only our ability to work hard stays with us.

In my personal view, if you are working hard and sincerely each day, even the divine intervenes and hugs you with an opportunity, and that is called luck! If you have an opportunity to work hard and choose to work harder, consider yourself the luckiest because it makes you utilize yourself. Wealth is a result of luck. You could work your hardest and make pennies, or you could work hard for a few months and end up with enormous wealth. We should not hold the idea of wealth so dearly; it's not in our hands. Only what we do truly is.

An everyday ability to push oneself to exercise, tidy up, or be positive is hard work, but it leads to small (but great) results. Hard work is a great way to keep the devils of your mind at bay, and when they are away, angels manifest themselves within you to develop angelic goals. If you have a goal, then the final result is a sequence of everyday goals you set for yourself to bring you closer to your end result.

We run away from working hard because our dreams scare us instead of getting us excited. We do not get excited because the devil within us does not want to be homeless, and we get too comfortable with our shortcomings. Everything purposeful requires effort, and the irony of life is that hard work in itself is a purpose, a success, and a positive reinforcement in life. It occupies our brain and shuts off irrelevant thoughts so we can focus only on the relevant ones.

You don't have to have your life figured out right in this moment, but you do have to figure out what you are going to with the resources and time you have. Decide what you are ready for and what you're capable of doing in the moments that come next . . .

Chapter Thirteen

Self-Dependence

"The stupid neither forgive nor forget; the naive forgive and forget; the wise forgive but do not forget."
— *Thomas Szasz*

Human connections are extremely fragile; one minute, you could be loved and admired, and the next, you could be seen as a villain in someone's life. We spend so much of our energy and effort pleasing people that we create an expectation that others should reciprocate our effort. When that expectation is broken, we feel hurt, and it causes a dent in our personality and mindset.

The mechanism to cope with emotional pain comes from within. We get over it because time and life take up so much space in our minds that everything eventually gets brushed under in our subconscious. It's in our nature to heal with time. The question is, why do others easily sideline us and our emotions from their lives? It's because every person is living their own reality and they may honour what they like and understand.

Hey, there's nothing wrong with that. Everyone is looking out for what they can afford, what makes them happy, and what kind of a person they would like to be. We expect our corporate bosses to be kind to us, but we forget that their main goals are to keep their job and drive up profits. Some of them may not be looking out for their employees, and if they can find a better "yes-man" candidate, everyone else becomes disposable. We idolize famous people, but we forget we have no role to play in their reality. It's easy to get too attached to them and follow them mindlessly.

Relationships are based on the idea of giving. The moment we expect something is the moment our heart will break because we expect the other person to be the way we would like them to be. This expectation isn't fair when it's sprung upon us; we don't want to feel obligated to do something that doesn't make us happy or isn't our way.

At our core, everyone wants to do things for themselves in their own way, including us. Everyone is living in their own created reality, working through their own challenges, and we must seek learnings from everyone to help us be more resilient. The moments of silence that speak the loudest are times when we should be aware conscientiously and remember that we have the power to be in high spirits and captain this ship even in turbulent waters!

Positive Reinforcement from Within

As I grew older and away from many people I had known, those people messaged me conveying my impact on their lives, the good and the bad. I found out that some people I did not even consider as my friends had immense grudges against me. Others, I discovered, held me in high regard. I never did that deliberately. Some people just weren't as important to me as I was to them.

At times, we go to a restaurant or coffee shop where front-line workers are rude and frustrated. We label them as unfit for the job when we might have no idea that they are having a bad day or have been mistreated by their boss or a customer. Everyone lives in their own state of mind. When we constantly expect others to interact with us positively, we set up our minds to lose control. We depend on others for positive reinforcement, and depending on how others treat us or behave with us, that's how we derive our self-worth. Of course, one would expect to live in a society where people are polite and courteous, but frustrations get the best of human character.

When we get sick, no matter what others do for us, they can never feel our discomfort. When we get hurt in a relationship, no one else can feel our mind's inability to replace that hurt. Yes, they might empathize momentarily, but eventually, they will move on with living their lives, and we are the ones who end up with that broken feeling. Only we can put in the effort and time to heal our wounded self. No one else can do that for us. It's like eating and expecting another person to do the loo business for us.

We worry so much about what others think of us that we don't realize that they have to deal with their own challenges. They don't have time or space in their minds to give us any regard. I was sitting in class once, and a handsome dude walked in late, interrupting the professor's lecture. He was embarrassed, but it didn't even cross my mind that he was causing an interruption. Instead, I thought to myself, "Ooh, what a nice-looking lad and why am I looking like a hobo today?"

The idea of stage fright, walking in late to a classroom, or dressing up for a party, seems so much bigger in our heads than it actually is. Everyone dresses up and cleans up nice for a party, and everyone is worried about looking good themselves. We let the anticipation of what others will think affect us so much that we forget to be secure and confident in our own skin.

We always want to wear the trendiest outfit and own the trendiest things. We end up with a giant pile of clothes, and yet we only pick that same comfortable T-shirt to wear whenever we can. The idea of deriving our self-worth from others is futile because no one really can create those emotions within us. The more we chase the need of being liked and understood by others, the further we will drive ourselves insane; it's never going to happen, and it should be irrelevant.

Will Power

"It is folly for a man to pray to the gods for that which he has the power to obtain by himself." —Epicurus

When we lose a loved one, we undermine our power of coping with the loss. Eventually, we have no choice but to get up and feed ourselves so we can survive. When economic depression hits, we undermine our ability to pick up any job to feed ourselves and keep a roof over our heads. Our body can fight just about any injury or disease, but we forget that we have the tools within us to fight through just about anything in life.

We can easily lift our spirits by reading a book to create positive changes. Instead, we get lured by the comfort of reacting from our instant emotions. Many folks who are enrolled in universities struggle to study and pass exams because it requires a lot of self-discipline, hard work, and focus. Those are the only ingredients needed to make us pass an exam. The ability to push ourselves to study and not binge-watch a TV show makes us realize that whatever we need to pass that exam is within us. It is us tuning our minds to focus on our desired result. It is our willpower.

We are tremendously powerful and can create a capacity to work, cope with hurt, and heal ourselves.

We can choose to partake in positive activities to fill our time and minds. When we wear a nice outfit, we feel good about the way we look. When we accomplish a task, we feel good about our abilities.

Our ability to work hard to pass an exam only gets accelerated as the exam date or deadline approaches. We use all the forces and strength within us to study, and we feel so relieved once we get through it. With time, when our emotional hurt declines, we feel so light and responsible for making peace with our baggage. No one is going to pay our bills for us, no one is going to digest our food for us, no one is going to sleep for us, and no one is going to write an exam for us. No one can make us realize our self-worth, make us confident, or unconditionally love us. We are the only ones responsible for all the shots that we miss.

The power to heal and the power to do is within ourselves. We create frustration by allowing our fear of putting in work to get in the way of our dreams. We have everything we need to control our moods, feelings, future, and relationships. However, our acknowledgement of this gets misled by fear because we spend too much time questioning our self-identity and abilities. When fear takes over, we only go further from being self-reliant and fulfilled within.

After a breakup, we may pour our hearts out on social media for attention. We love to be understood and feel others' sympathy. It makes us feel that our excuses are valid and that our victim mindset must continue for us to be treated favourably by others. The

child in all of us expects the same emotional pamper-
ing that we got as a child from our parents and caretak-
ers. We waste time hoping others will understand us
by swimming in a pity pool while wanting others to
uplift us.

Staying in a mindset that is contingent on the
behaviour of others will only result in disappointment
because no one can truly walk in our shoes. The quicker
we realize that we are the only ones who can nourish
ourselves, the less time we will spend getting frustrated.
Smokers try to quit smoking with many methods, like
patches or gum, but they can never be successful until
they learn to control their urge to smoke. We have all
it takes within us to cope with whatever life throws at
us. The less we focus on that, the harder it will be to
utilize our power within. Our life is unique to us, and
we have to find our own unique way of living it.

Trust Nature's Hurdles

For a middle-class child, the hurdles at home might
be the freedom to watch endless television. For a child
growing up on the streets, the struggle might be food
and survival. Everyone's struggle is different, and so
is everyone's ability to deal with it. The Mr. Sun that
some enjoy tanning their skin under might be despised
by others because it burns their leather! A challenge to
others might not be a challenge for us. It doesn't make
us better, and it does not mean others are lacking. We

are all cut out for different challenges. Yes, some people are supremely petty and possessive of little things because they don't have faith and awareness in the abundance of this vast universe, so we must remember to not become like them and narrow our vision. The burden of disappointment is something we have in our hands to off-load our shoulders. Don't confine yourself to being jaded by the pettiness of others; change the thought and topic. Don't overthink everything. Don't try to understand it deeply as there is nothing deep behind it. It is simply shallow and has a miserable human behind the action. Bless them with the strength to find happiness in other meaningful things. Move on by seeing the abundance in your life.

When we face setbacks, we must realize our bodies and ourselves have the power to overcome them. You must not waste time getting frustrated and becoming your own hurdle. The sooner we embrace that we are the only ones who can help ourselves, the quicker we will realize the importance of being self-dependent.

We cannot control how others are, but we can control the aspects of our lives, our home, our food, our body, our efforts, and how we interact with others. We must acknowledge that we are in control of what happens to us. We are the ones creating what happens, and the sooner we acknowledge that, the better it would be for us. We can face a hurdle and work on it to overcome it or be defined by being a victim of the hurdle.

We only face struggles that we can handle. Nothing given to us—good or bad—is outside of the laws of nature. Ability is unique to everyone. Cactus grows in the desert, and palms grow near a water body. We only acquire struggles that enable us to work a specific muscle. We don't get anything out of order. Everything is in perfect synchronicity, and we can harness the power within. Laying around in self-pity or hoping for cosmic help is wasting time.

Success comes from working through our setbacks. If you can spend your days meeting what life demands of you, then you are truly helping yourself. Everything else is just waiting for time to pass by. Everything we need, we have within ourselves. All the love, support, and courage we need is discoverable if we acknowledge willpower's ability. If your mind places enough emphasis on self-improvement, the rest are just gifts. That's when you become self-reliant.

You don't need anyone to make you feel good about yourself or to approve of you. It is easier to be the one who is good to others instead. Everyone is choosing their own reality. We have to acknowledge that we are in charge of choosing ours too. We must use our time to do things that make us feel good and happy rather than looking for it in others.

When we spend and save based on our income, we create opportunities for ourselves to feel a sense of security. When we live to compete with others or spend based on our wants rather than our needs, we are bound to end up in debt, often labouring for years to pay it back.

We must accept what is and focus on what we can do with our abilities in our present circumstances. We are more powerful than we know. We must believe in our power to handle whatever life throws at us with our tools of pragmatism and our goals of self-preservation. Our self-dependence relies on our ability to be practical, which we must practice with ourselves. You can never depend on yourself if nothing you do is about you or authentic to you.

Chapter Fourteen

New Dawn Within

To see the beauty at sunrise, we must be awake and ready right before dawn. Just before the sun is about to rise, the birds start chirping, nature starts waking up, and traffic noise starts to creep in. We must wake up before the world glows to truly see and feel the beauty and magic of our world as the light spreads across.

Similarly, to see a substantial change outside of us, we must wire ourselves on the inside to manifest the world's beauty and our diamond-like human life. Every day is an opportunity to begin anew with a clean state of mind and the ability to write your own rules and create your own reality. Of course, we will all fumble and tumble some days, but we must also remember our ability to cope with things and move forward. The truth is, as humans, we all are stricken with many problems of our health, life, and mind. Each one of us has and is going through an existential crisis. We all want to feel purposeful while racing against time, and we all fall down. But it is acknowledgement toward the power of every new day that brings opportunities to keep striving and improving that we can seize.

We must surrender to how beautiful and beyond our intelligence nature is. Everything is in perfect order, and we are not alone on this planet. We must align ourselves to the laws of nature to feel at home. Everyday practice makes this a habit. Our past is only an awareness of who we are and what has led us to today. If we repeat the same mindset in our present, then no wonder the outcome will repeat itself. When we accept nature for how it is, we align ourselves with those forces until we become a force of nature ourselves.

We possess the powerful tool of acceptance, which allows us to live in utmost surrender and gratitude. During a solar eclipse (when a shadow is cast on earth by the moon intercepting the sun), we see the sun for about eight minutes after the eclipse takes place. This is because it takes eight minutes for sunlight to travel the 149 million miles of space to reach our eyes. Light travels at approximately 300,000 km per second, which is known as the speed of light.

Some stars we see today may not even be present in the sky because it takes millions of years for their light to reach our eyes. When a star that is millions of light-years away dies, we will only know for sure when a million light-years have passed. What we think exists might not even exist in reality, and it might just be what we see in the moment. When we dream in our sleep, it all seems real—the fear, the emotions, the happiness, and the mishaps. Life is nothing but a dream and we by default are sleeping until we choose to wake up and free ourselves from our own selves. One way or the other, the dream will be over, and we will all have to wake up, so why spend a beautiful dream by not dreaming the dream we want to dream?

Set Expectations for Yourself

Our brain is the most intelligent thing that we possess. We must always use it to create and see things that bring us true enlightenment and peace. It's not our partner or our family who will reap the benefits of our positive mindset. It is first and foremost us who will attract goodness from the world if we become good ourselves.

Life is too short and too long to wait for our expectations to be fulfilled by others. We can have expectations, but we should first have them of ourselves. We should gauge our success rate by analyzing if we met our own expectations for what we are currently experiencing and feeling. We aren't doing anyone a favour by being alive. We are living because it is the command of the cosmos, and we must respect and accept that first.

We must use our abilities to live without the entanglement of our emotions, greed, or jealousy. Our life is our one chance to be the best version of ourselves. If you want to be liked by people, like people first. If you want to be loved, love first. If you want to be healthy, live a healthy lifestyle first, and if you want to be successful, you have to put in the hard work first.

Acceptance, compassion, and love are the fuel that you need to live in high spirits. Be present in the moment and see all that you are blessed with, no matter what life's circumstances may be. Even an imperfect situation will seem perfect. Open your eyes to see opportunities in every situation.

I used to have interpersonal problems with people I was close to. I would expect them to behave the way I wanted them to behave or say things that would make me feel good. Those expectations caused a ruckus inside me until I could no longer go on living in my mental cage. There comes a time when we first have to change ourselves. We must first sacrifice our ego, expectations, ideas, and perceptions to understand someone else's. Only then will we manifest any fruitful change on the inside. If you are unhappy with who you are and how your life is in the current moment, then know it is something inside you that manifested that. You are wholly responsible for it.

We all want to chase success and riches, but please know that all the wealthy businessmen are somewhat shrewd and have stepped over someone to get where they are. All they care about is accumulating more as though it was never enough in the first place, and it never will be, not just in terms of money, but everything else too. If that is what life should be about—being greedy, stepping over people, being possessive about some gold coins, and abusing relationships—then perhaps it's time to rethink your idea of success. The irony is that it's because of these money-grabbing businessmen that most people in the world earn their wages, which is what keeps the economy going. Somewhere, we all are a part of this unwilling cycle, and we don't have the right to blame one entity or the other. The only thing we can do is accept everyone as they are and exhibit the best of us toward people and nature.

Respect Your Destiny

Life is 90% destiny and is based on what our cosmos has drawn for us. We need to understand that our life cannot sustain us on its own. It exists because of natural forces like gravity, the atmosphere we breathe in, the earth we live on, and a decade of evolution. As children, we do not have control of what we wear, eat, or which school we will study at. It is laid out for us, and we don't have to stop our engines constantly to figure out the unknown. The best we can do is flow with it, and life itself unlocks those answers for us.

However, 10% of our life is our free will. We can control our emotions and what we choose to do with what we have. It's up to us to make something negative into the greatest blessing of our life based on how we choose to run with it. Painting a sorry picture of yourself or being vindicated by everything is only causing self-harm. It is not hurting anyone else but you. It will not make you lovable. Instead, you'll become a burden.

You should still be aware of people who have less than you. Challenges and adversaries are a natural part of living. We have manifested all the experiences that we are going through. God has blessed us with the opportunity to pour magic into everything with our love and our ability to create.

I used to work with a visually disabled person in my university who one day asked me, "How does the colour blue look? Is it more toward the black or white spectrum of the colour scheme?" I was puzzled about how to answer that because there are so many dark and light shades of blue that it can be a whole colour chart. It made me realize that a billion dollars could not match the priceless senses we are blessed with. That lady worked hard, lived by herself, got her nails done, and suggested solutions for visually impaired students. She was a beautiful singer and never made herself a victim of any prejudice. She had never had a serious or intimate relationship and wasn't miserable compared to people whose only cry in life is to find love. I was truly ashamed of myself for not being grateful for every little gift I had been blessed with. Frankly, it opened my eyes to see the power of our will. Even though most of us have the power to see, we still choose to remain blind.

Patience Leads to Rewards

A magical life is indeed possible, but it requires patience and effort. When I took up my major at university, I had not thought of any career prospects that could come out of it. I ended up working in an unrelated field and eventually got let go. Instead of looking for a new job, I decided to work on myself. I wanted to make myself capable of pursuing other avenues for a stream of income and also write my two cents in a book.

While writing, I realized how lucky I am to have studied in the faculty of social sciences. It exposed me to the world of philosophy and taught me about different ideologies. Also, cooking for so many years made me realize that I can work in the food industry. I can generate income while being my own boss. For the first time, I actually like what I was doing.

Sometimes, it is hard to understand why something is happening or why we have what we have in the moment. We're usually anxious about the future. However, nothing is happening out of order. We are exactly where we are supposed to be. It's up to us to choose whether we will let something numb us or choose to keep doing what we can to keep moving forward productively.

No relationships, careers, or materials hold the key to being present and living our lives. It is only our intention and our willpower to find peace and make the best of each day. Having discipline or daily commitments, like waking up early to go for a walk or eating right, can bring us closer to ourselves and make us hold ourselves accountable. No one can be in high spirits every day. Sometimes, a negative experience can deflate us, but if we have certain commitments to ourselves or a rule that we follow, we can ignite self-love and do whatever it takes to move forward. We also try to be too perfect. There is no such thing as being perfect. All we can do is try to be balanced in life. We can do that by dealing with each situation or a person with the best of our ability. Respecting other people and giving them the freedom to be themselves is also a way to treat others the best you can. Helping others when you have first helped yourself is how we can pay back. The more we focus on striking a balance, there more at ease, we will be able to feel. Do the best in any circumstance, be generous, be sincere, and that is a way to feel content with yourself. All we can really do is try our best in our own little way possible. While working the muscle of trying to be balanced, the power of detachment should also not be neglected. The way to relax one's mind is to live in the moment. To be in the moment, we must actively detach from other noises in our heads and be fully participating and present to the best of our ability. Only then will each moment of life be cherished and lived. Living in the moment results from either shedding the overthinking by working out, waking up early, staying up late, or having a good session of sitting still and quietly, breathing deeply, and without distractions in one place

It takes practice, and it takes effort. Nothing comes easy, and if it did, we wouldn't value it as much. Some days will be amazing, some boring, some depressing, some very busy, and some will be full of different experiences. They all shall pass. Like good days pass, bad days and times won't last forever. It's all a part of the journey, and the only person living through it all is you.

You and your attitude are the only constant things in life. Life does not stop for anyone, and it ends the same for everyone. We cannot just let a problem take over our life or allow good days to hypnotize us. Good and bad doesn't mean anything when your spirit is always accepting and content with who you are.

A good conversation can change our mindset overnight, and one good day at work can make us feel appreciated. Similarly, we can lose our loved ones or ourselves overnight. All the daily in-betweens, no matter how strenuous or joyful, shouldn't be taken too seriously. Every day we wake up, we have a chance to live in a way that serves us and to go to bed self-reflecting and hopeful. It takes patience, and it takes time to see results.

Trust Nature's Order

We don't need to know everything right now. To do this, we go to tarot card readers or astrologers, but no one can really predict our future. Even if they can, it has no significance if we are not present enough to live it. Being aware and putting our best foot forward only does us good. Even if tangible or visual goods do not manifest, we at least feel good about our life. We truly lived each day by adding meaning to our life by bringing some fulfillment instead of just watching it pass us by.

We need to let go of the idea that we control everything; we don't. We don't control the approximately seven billion people and twenty quintillion animals on this earth. We don't control life cycles or the air we breathe. The only thing we control is what we choose our minds to see and pursue. If we are constantly looking for sadness, then we will only find sadness. If we find reasons to be happy, then we will only find ourselves in situations that bring joy to our lives. That is the law of attraction; we attract the feeling that we behold.

You cannot control what happened in the past or what will happen in the future. You do control how your day is going and where you want it to head toward. Days become years, and years become decades that become centuries. The power of each day should not be undermined by the fear of tomorrow.

It takes practice and slow progress instead of holding ourselves to exceptionally high standards. The frustration and inability of holding ourselves accountable to a very drastic change every day are unrealistic. The first step we can take toward our inner journey to alignment is simply taking a few deep breaths.

Attitude of Gratitude

Life is truly a gift that won't last forever. It is our responsibility to add happiness to each day. Every day is the youngest you'll ever be and the oldest you have ever been. Each day is a new day and a new chance to live or see things that bring a smile to your face, whether it's by eating a good meal or asking a distant relative how they are.

Don't rush or become desperate to be in a "perfect" situation. Every stage and state of life comes with its own internal and external challenges. If we are truly living our present the best way possible, we can create a stable life. It will be contingent on ourselves, and that is something no one can take away from us. Only we can predict for ourselves with the utmost reliability.

I had read many books and texts about gratitude and thought it just meant mindlessly being grateful for what we have. We can say "thank you" out loud for the things we have, but if we have taken things for granted and never fully optimized everything we have, we are not grateful in our intentions. Our behaviours and our words are a direct reflection of who we are on the inside. If you are mindlessly saying negative words out loud, then it shows what is inside of you. That should be your first indication that you are creating something that isn't going to serve you in the long run.

When we can't control our present, we have no chance whatsoever to control our future. It is our responsibility to see the good in every day and to pick up the next day from where we left off. If we focus on playing our part right and being grateful for every person and everything that we have, it will uplift us and those around us. We will then find people who are on the same journey and have experiences that will only enhance our lives instead of inviting mediocrity.

By making excuses or blaming others, we are only wasting our time on feelings and thoughts that don't make us live today and this very moment. Time does not stop for anyone, and nor should you.

Live Every Day

I decided to write this book because everyday life experiences helped me make sense of the chaos within. I feel abundant because of every lesson that God helped me carve out. Life is nothing but a bunch of stories told in different ways and the same things done in different manners. Others, and specifically those around me, helped me become the better me for my own good. I hope sharing my wisdom can help you feel not alone on this beautiful yet messy journey. Many others are fighting the inner battle just like you and me. When we truly seek help, it does arrive for us.

There is no perfect method to life, but it is simply our everyday mindset that gives meaning and some direction to the mundane. The dawn of the day kicks off unhurriedly, but the light gets brighter as time passes. Eventually, dusk transforms into extreme darkness due to the absence of light. The more we let the light of the new dawn within take over, the brighter we will live. If we let the darkness and absence of light seep inside us, the more lost in the darkness we will become.

We are all connected to the same sources of life: the air, the sun, the earth, the moon, and the laws that govern our universe. It is our responsibility to be better so the lives that we touch can become better. The chain then continues further. It is solely up to us to raise the level of living in the world by doing our part, bit by bit. We live in the reality that we create for ourselves, and we truly are the masters of our destiny, which is beyond death. We don't have to know what that is now. We'll surely cross that bridge when it's time.

"All darkness vanished when I saw the lamp within my heart." –Saint Kabir

*Thank you for letting me be
a part of your beautiful journey.*

.